THE WORK OF CHRIST

THERE HAVE BEEN MANY BOOKS DEVOTED TO INDIVIDUAL ASPECTS of the work of Christ, and in particular to His death upon the cross. One of the distinctive features of this book is that it sums up the teaching of the New Testament on the work of Christ as a whole, so that His death is seen in the context of His earthly life, His resurrection and exaltation, and His future coming. Dr Marshall's method is to consider the teaching of Jesus and then to survey the New Testament writers in turn, so that the reader may be able to trace something of the development of New Testament theology. At the same time, the essential unity of the New Testament is demonstrated, as each writer is seen to bear his own characteristic witness to the revelation of salvation in Jesus Christ. A final chapter poses the question whether modern theology and evangelism can still use the language of the New Testament in describing the work of Christ.

Dr Marshall was Assistant Tutor at Didsbury Methodist College (now Wesley College), Bristol, and a Methodist minister in Darlington before coming to his present post as Lecturer in New Testament Exegesis in the University of Aberdeen.

THE WORK OF CHRIST
I. HOWARD MARSHALL

Ronald N. Haynes Publishers, Inc.
PALM SPRINGS CALIFORNIA

THE WORK OF CHRIST

Copyright © 1969, 1981 by I. HOWARD MARSHALL

Ronald N. Haynes Publishers, Inc.
Palm Springs, California 92263

First USA Edition 1981

LIBRARY OF CONGRESS CATALOG CARD NUMBER: 81-83169
ISBN 0-88021-018-4

Printed in the United States of America

Originally published by
THE PATERNOSTER PRESS
PATERNOSTER HOUSE
3 MOUNT RADFORD CRESENT
EXETER UK EX2 4JW
ENGLAND

Contents

Preface

THIS BRIEF SURVEY OF THE WORK OF CHRIST HAS ARISEN FROM the conviction that there is a need for a book which will attempt to present within a short compass the New Testament teaching about the significance of Christ's work as a whole. Most authors have confined their attention to one particular aspect of the subject, such as the death or resurrection of Christ, or have produced a historical survey of His earthly ministry. The present writer's aim has been to summarize the theological interpretation of the whole work of Christ as it is seen in the various parts of the New Testament.

It can be argued that the main interest of the New Testament writers was in the *work* of Christ rather than in His *person* as such. If this is so, the present work may be seen as an introduction to the central theme of New Testament theology.

In order to make the book suitable for as wide a readership as possible, an attempt has been made to keep the presentation on a simple level. Discussion of problems of interpretation has been avoided, and footnotes kept to a minimum. Many points in the text require much fuller substantiation than is possible within such limits, but to have provided such technical detail would have completely altered the purpose and character of the present book.

A word of thanks is due to a number of friends whose comments on the manuscript have helped to purge it of many shortcomings. A word of apology is also due. In 1910 the distinguished theologian P. T. Forsyth published his notable study of the atonement entitled *The Work of Christ*. It proved impossible to discover a simple title which would describe the contents of the present book more adequately than that already used by P. T. Forsyth, and the writer trusts that he may be pardoned for adopting the phrase made famous by him to introduce his own modest contribution to the same great subject.

I. HOWARD MARSHALL

December, 1968

One

Introduction

A FAMOUS BOOK OF HALF A CENTURY OR SO AGO BY W. H. GRIFFITH Thomas had as its title *Christianity is Christ.* The statement made in that title is sufficient to show that it is somewhat rash to entitle this slim volume *The Work of Christ,* for the theme to be expounded is as wide as Christianity itself and sums up the central message of the New Testament.

Traditionally, to be sure, our title has had a somewhat limited reference. It has been understood to refer particularly to the doctrine of the death of Christ; the celebrated work of P. T. Forsyth written under this same title had as its theme the atonement made by Christ on the cross for the sins of mankind. But too narrow a preoccupation with the few brief hours of the first Good Friday and Easter Sunday would fail to do justice to a theme which stretches from eternity to eternity. It begins at the moment when the Father created the worlds through His Son and appointed Him as heir (Heb. 1: 2), and it reaches its consummation when the Son, His work completed, hands over His rule to the Father and enjoys with His people the glory of heaven for evermore (1 Cor. 15:24). Even if the first Christians made the death and resurrection of Jesus the centre of their preaching (1 Cor. 15:3–5), they could not remain content with this delimitation of their message for very long, and soon they began to tell what He had done during His earthly life and what He was destined to do in the future.

It is not too easy to reduce such a broad theme to a manageable compass. At first glance, it might seem best to gather together the teaching given about the work of Christ in the New Testament and to arrange it chronologically, that is to say, to begin in eternity past and to expound in consecutive order all that Christ has done since then and all that He will do in the future. The difficulty is that this would produce a rather ill-balanced story. It would be rather like the political biography of some modern statesman whose early years and retirement are treated with great brevity in comparison with the few vital years during which he held high office. It is no disparagement of the other aspects of the work of Christ to say that for the Christian the greatest significance is attached to His earthly life, and in particular to a few days at its conclusion. The amount of space devoted by the biblical writers to the death and exaltation of Jesus is so utterly disproportionate in comparison with that devoted to other aspects of His work that a chronological arrangement of our study would be of little help in dividing up and classifying the material; it might even lead us to miss the central theme of the New Testament message.

We would do better, therefore, to consider the work of Christ from a topical point of view. This would mean collecting and analysing the different aspects under which the New Testament writers see His work. A good example of this approach is found in E. Stauffer's *New Testament Theology* (1955). This author considers the various themes of New Testament theology from three different points of view. From the *doxological* aspect the work of Christ is regarded as being performed for the glory (Gk. *doxa*) of God. The *antagonistic* point of view sees His work as being directed against the opposing powers of evil. The *soteriological* point of view observes how the work of Christ was carried through "for us men and for our salvation (Gk. *soteria*)". Thus the work of Christ is seen in relation to the three persons or groups of persons affected by it – God, the powers of evil and mankind. This is a most suggestive approach, and it is worth bearing in mind as we pursue our study.

Professor Stauffer himself draws his material from all parts of the New Testament without discrimination as he examines each aspect of New Testament theology from these three points of view. He presupposes that the various writers of the New Testament held a common faith and a common theology, and therefore he regards himself as justified in this eclectic approach to his subject.

We believe that this is a legitimate and helpful method of study, but it is open to the danger of too easily assimilating the ideas of the various New Testament writers to each other and of obscuring their different approaches to their theme. We propose, therefore, to adopt a different method, namely to examine in turn the thought of Jesus Himself and of the various New Testament witnesses to His work. This approach is the one suggested to us by the structure of the New Testament as we have it today. After telling the story of the life and ministry of Jesus in the Gospels, it goes on to describe the preaching and evangelism of the earliest Christians in the Acts of the Apostles, and then it presents us with documents which show how great Christian thinkers, including Peter, Paul, John and the unknown writer to the Hebrews, expressed their mature understanding of the work of Christ. By proceeding in this way we shall be able to do justice to the individual insights of the New Testament authors and to see how each of them regarded the work of Christ as a whole.

One or two comments must be made before we proceed to our study. First, as has just been indicated, the adoption of this method does not mean that there is in our opinion considerable divergence among the New Testament writers in their understanding of the work of Christ. In his important book *The Unity of the New Testament* (1943) Professor A. M. Hunter presented a powerful case that "there is . . . a deep unity in the New Testament, which dominates and transcends all the diversities".[1] He argued that the New Testament writers bear witness to one Lord, one Church and (what especially concerns us) one Salvation. We hope to show that there are good grounds for this judgement so far as the work of Christ is concerned. At many points Christian thinkers found themselves in full agreement on the significance of the work of Christ, even to the point of using the same vocabulary to describe it. Often they may express their doctrine in different ways, using different forms of speech and presentation, but it is the *same* doctrine that they all express. James Denney could rightly say that the inspiration of the Bible was to be seen in its unity as a testimony to God's sin-bearing love.[2]

A second point is that when we think in terms of the development of doctrine there is a temptation to suppose that complex ideas are always preceded by more simple ones and that it must be possible, at least in theory, to work out a plausible cause-and-effect line of development from the earliest to the latest ideas.

While this may be true of many epochs of human thought, it is not self-evident that it is always the case. There are plenty of examples of great men who have lived, as we say, 'before their time', and whose thought is not to be explained in terms of simple evolution. At the beginning of New Testament thought stands the figure of Jesus Himself. Unless we are prepared to deny that He had

[1]Op. cit., p. 109.
[2]*The Death of Christ* (1951), p. 174.

powers of insight greater than those of ordinary men, we are bound to say that a simple, evolutionary development is ruled out; the process of Christian thought begins with the sayings of a creative genius whom later thinkers could not match. Even to put the matter in this way will seem singularly inept and inadequate to Christian readers who believe that Jesus was the Son of God. It is not simply a case of an unusual man who out-thought His contemporaries; we are faced by a divine revelation at the beginning of the process. Moreover, this activity continued throughout the New Testament period as the various writers were illumined by the Holy Spirit and inspired to a more than human understanding of the significance of Jesus (see Jn. 14: 26; 16: 12–15; Eph. 3: 2–6). An attempt to 'trace the history of thought' regarding the work of Christ in the same way as one might attempt an evolutionary study of the development of Greek philosophy or of modern computer science is doomed to failure because it tries to handle in purely human categories something which altogether transcends them. In studying New Testament theology we are not dealing with a merely human phenomenon; it is shot through with divine inspiration.

A third point which arises is that since our documents describing the life of Jesus and the rise of the early Church were written some time after the events described, there is a difference, at least in principle, between the events as they actually happened and the way in which the writers described them. Modern scholarship has shown that the writers of the Gospels were theologians every bit as much as Paul or Peter, and that their writings provide evidence for their own theology as well as for the teaching of Jesus. Consequently, it is urged, it is extremely difficult, if not impossible, to work our way back to what Jesus actually said and did from what the Gospel writers later thought that He had said and done.[8]

In raising this matter we come up against one of the most complex problems in modern biblical study. In a treatment on the present scale it is impossible to do more than simply state a position with regard to it. Our belief is that, just as Paul and Peter express their common faith from different viewpoints, so the Gospel writers present individual pictures of Jesus which are complementary rather than contradictory. Further, there is good reason to suppose that the religious and theological ideas of the Evangelists, and of their

[8]For a survey of this approach see J. Rohde, *Rediscovering the Teaching of the Evangelists* (1969).

various predecessors to whom they were indebted for their information, were in fundamental harmony with those of Jesus Himself.[4] What the Evangelists were trying to do was to present the life and teaching of Jesus in a manner that would be intelligible to their generation and – under divine providence – to us. This is something quite different from saying that the effect of their work was rather to obscure what Jesus really said and did. It is true that a powerful body of scholarly opinion, headed in our own time by Rudolf Bultmann, would deny the historical value of the Gospels pretty radically, but we are prepared to take our stand with those scholars who hold that the essential reliability of the Gospels can be cogently defended.[5]

We may pinpoint the issue by reference to one particular aspect of it. It is well known that there are very considerable differences in atmosphere between the teaching of Jesus in the first three Gospels and that recorded in the Gospel of John. Many scholars have concluded that John may well have recorded his own inspired meditations on the words of Jesus rather than the actual words of Jesus Himself. Both conservative and radical scholars agree that the teaching of Jesus in this Gospel has passed through the crucible of John's own mind before crystallizing out in its present form; the difference between them concerns the degree to which the actual words of Jesus may be found in John. There is, however, a growing opinion that the traditions recorded in John have as much right to be regarded as historical as those in the other Gospels.[6] In view of this, it has seemed right to us to use evidence from the Gospel of John in our discussion of the teaching of Jesus. What is uncertain from time to time is whether such quotations give the very words of Jesus or the inspired comment of the Evangelist upon His message. This holds true both for the Gospel of John (where the problem is most acute) and for the first three Gospels. From the point of view of historical study, it is not unimportant to be able to decide between two possibilities, but in the context of the present introduction to New Testament teaching where our primary aim is to expound what the New Testament actually says, individual questions of authenticity have not been raised. We believe, however, that the texts to be

---

[4]See C. E. B. Cranfield, *The Gospel according to St Mark* (1963²), pp. 16, 479.
[5]See, for example, Carl F. H. Henry (ed.), *Jesus of Nazareth: Saviour and Lord* (1967).
[6]A. M. Hunter, *According to John* (1968).

cited provide an essentially reliable guide to the teaching of Jesus regarding His own work, whether or not the actual wording is His in every case.

We propose, therefore, to commence with the Gospels in order to discover Jesus' own concept of His work. From that beginning, expounded in the next chapter, we shall go on to examine in turn the various ways in which the early Church and its leading figures formed a comprehensive doctrine of His work. A final section will consider the significance of the New Testament teaching as a whole for today.

Two

Jesus and His Mission

SHORTLY BEFORE HE DIED, JESUS TOOK HIS CLOSEST FRIENDS INTO A garden outside Jerusalem and in their presence He prayed to God. He was conscious of the impending suffering that He must face, and in His deep distress of soul He confessed His desire that the 'cup' of suffering and divine wrath which He was about to drink might be taken from Him. Then He added the significant words, "Yet not what I will, but what thou wilt" (Mk. 14: 36). In this single sentence there is summed up the formal character of the work of Jesus. He came to do the will of God His Father. The fact that He found His deepest satisfaction in so doing is expressed in His saying, "My food is to do the will of him who sent me, and to accomplish his work" (Jn. 4: 34). The writer to the Hebrews very aptly puts the words of Psalm 40: 7–8 upon the lips of Christ as He came into this world: "Then I said, 'Lo, I have come to do thy will, O God', as it is written of me in the roll of the book" (Heb. 10: 7).

In making obedience to the will of God the aim of His life Jesus was simply fulfilling the responsibilities attached to His person. In the Gospels He frequently spoke of God as His Father and, less frequently, of Himself as the Son of God (e.g. Mt. 11: 25–27; Mk. 13: 32).[1] When we use the words 'father' and 'son', it is probably the thought of physical relationship which is uppermost in our minds. It is not so certain that the Jews thought in quite the same way; thoughts of fatherly care and filial obedience characterized the relationship for them. Oscar Cullman can say, "The Old Testament and Jewish concept of the Son of God is essentially characterized, not by the gift of a particular power, nor by a substantial relationship with God by virtue of divine conception; but by the idea of *election* to participation in divine work through the execution of a particular commission, and by the idea of strict *obedience* to the God who

[1]For the authenticity of this aspect of the teaching of Jesus see I. H. Marshall, 'The Divine Sonship of Jesus', *Interpretation* 21 (1967), pp. 87–103.

elects".[2] The idea is expressed in the word of God through Isaiah as
He bitterly complains, "Sons have I reared and brought up, but they
have rebelled against me," and goes on to speak of "sons who deal
corruptly! They have forsaken the Lord" (Is. 1: 2, 4; cf. Ex. 4: 22 f.;
Mal. 3: 17 b).

It goes without saying that the Sonship of Jesus transcends the
categories of election and obedience in which the relationship of
Israel to God was expressed, but it remains true that as the Son of
God Jesus was supremely conscious of His duty of obedience to the
Father. As early as His 'coming of age' visit to the temple, He was
conscious that He must be 'in His Father's house' (Lk. 2: 49); the
older, but less likely rendering, 'about my Father's business', makes
the point more explicit. When the heavenly voice addressed Him at
His baptism with the words, "Thou art my beloved Son; with thee I
am well pleased" (Mk. 1: 11), the allusion to Is. 42: 1 shows that the
delight of God in His Son was because He was about to fulfil the task
of the Servant of the Lord. The way in which Jesus immediately
afterwards repulsed Satan with the quotation, "You shall worship
the Lord your God and him only shall you serve" (Mt. 4: 10, quoting
Dt. 6: 13; cf. Mt. 4: 4), shows that He had understood His baptism
as a call to obedient service of God. And when He later said, "Not
every one who says to me, 'Lord, Lord', shall enter the kingdom of
heaven, but he who does the will of my Father who is in heaven"
(Mt. 7: 22), we are fully entitled to conclude *a fortiori* that the One
who proclaimed the kingdom of heaven Himself practised such
obedience to the will of God; this is surely implicit also in the
saying about the condition for spiritual kinship with Jesus: "Whoever does the will of God is my brother, and sister, and mother"
(Mk. 3: 35).

The same point is reiterated in the Gospel of John. There we find
that Jesus spoke of Himself as one who did not seek His own will
but the will of Him who sent Him (Jn. 5: 3). He claimed that He did
nothing of His own accord but whatever He saw the Father doing
(Jn. 5: 19). "I have come down from heaven," He said, "not to do my
own will, but the will of Him who sent me" (Jn. 6: 38). And again, "I
do nothing on my own authority but speak thus as the Father taught
me. And He who sent me is with me; He has not left me alone, for I
always do what is pleasing to Him" (Jn. 8: 28 f.).[3]

[2]O. Cullman, *The Christology of the New Testament* (1959), p. 275.
[3]Cf. 10: 18; 12: 49–50; 14: 24, 31; 15: 10; 17: 4.

The Scriptural Pattern

If the general character of the work of Jesus can be summed up in terms of filial obedience to the will of the Father, we must now attempt to give some content to this formal statement. The expression of the Father's will which Jesus obeyed is to be found in the pattern appointed in the Scriptures of the Old Testament.

This is expressed in the most general way in the use of the word 'must' (Gk. *dei*) which indicates that a 'divine necessity' governed the activity of Jesus. We find that Jesus spoke in this way especially of His sufferings:[4] "He began to teach them that the Son of man must suffer many things, and be rejected . . ., and be killed, and after three days rise again" (Mk. 8: 31).[5] He also spoke of the necessity of being in His Father's house (Lk. 2: 29) and especially of His preaching the Gospel and bringing salvation to such a one as Zacchaeus (Lk. 4: 43; 19: 5). The same sense of divine constraint has been suspected in the 'must' which governed Jesus' journey to Samaria and His successful witness there (Jn. 4: 4), but the word here may simply refer to the necessity to pass through Samaria when travelling by the quickest route from Judea to Galilee.

There is clearly no reference here to a 'fate' which must be worked out and cannot be avoided. Nor is the reference to the necessities imposed by some kind of rigid, apocalyptic timetable. When Jesus used this word 'must', He was thinking of the will of God expressed in Scripture which imposed a divine constraint upon Him. As He anticipated His sufferings, Jesus said, "For I tell you that this scripture must be fulfilled in me, 'And he was reckoned with transgressors'; for what is written about me has its fulfilment" (Lk. 23: 37, quoting Is. 53: 12; cf. Lk. 24: 26 f., 44). In the Scriptures Jesus found the pattern of His life laid down for Him. He spoke of actions taking place 'as it has been written'; the phrase is in the perfect tense (Gk. *gegraptai*) which conveys the idea of a past action whose force

[4]J. Denney, *The Death of Christ*, p. 29.

[5]Cf. Lk. 13: 33; 17: 25; 24: 7, 26; Jn. 3: 14; 12: 34; 20: 9; Acts 17: 3, The prophecies of His own death by Jesus are regarded as inventions by the early church (*vaticinia post eventum*) by R. Bultmann, *Theology of the New Testament* (1952), I, p. 30. For a defence of the fact that Jesus reckoned with the possibility of His own violent death see J. Jeremias in G. Kittel (ed.), *Theological Dictionary of the New Testament* (1964–), V, pp. 713 f. (NOTE: The English translation of this work has so far reached Volume V. Where succeeding volumes are referred to, the references are to the original German edition.)

and validity remain into the present time. For Jesus, to say 'I must' and 'It stands written' were one and the same thing. So when the Son of man went forth from the supper table to be betrayed and crucified, the whole action is said to have taken place 'as it is written of him' (Mk. 14: 21), and the disciples left Him to face His enemies alone because, "it is written, 'I will strike the shepherd, and the sheep will be scattered' " (Mk. 14: 27). What was true of the general direction of Jesus' life was true also of details; frequently He justified the position which He adopted or the course of action which He recommended to His disciples or the people at large with an 'It is written' (e.g. Mt. 4: 4, 7; Mk. 11: 17). He referred to the course of John the Baptist's career in the same way (Mt. 11: 10; Mk. 9: 13), and the Evangelists were only following His example when they saw His ministry as taking place in accordance with what was written in Scripture (Mk. 1: 2).[6]

It is simply another way of making the same point to say that in the work of Jesus the prophetic Scriptures were fulfilled. Again the Passion story comes to mind. When the rabble seized Jesus to arrest Him like a robber or brigand, He asked them why they had not arrested Him peaceably when He was teaching in the temple; 'but,' He said, 'let the scriptures be fulfilled' (Mk. 14: 49; no specific Old Testament text appears to be in mind). This thought, that certain events in the life of Jesus fulfilled Scripture, is a very common one and is taken up by the Evangelists, especially by Matthew.[7]

Jesus the Prophet

Although we have now determined that the work of Jesus was governed by the will of God as expressed in the Scriptures, we have still to give some content to this general conception by asking in what precise ways Jesus saw Himself as fulfilling the Old Testament. We shall approach this question by considering the roles which Jesus felt Himself called to fulfil. He was conscious of being the One whom God had promised would come at the end of time to redeem His people.

At the simplest level this role was that of being the prophet of God. The fact that the people seriously asked whether He was a

[6]Cf. Mt. 2: 5; Jn. 1: 45; 2: 17; 12: 14, 16.
[7]E.g. Mt. 1: 22; 2: 15, 17, 23; 4: 14; Lk. 4: 21; 24: 44; Jn. 12: 38; 13: 18. See R. H. Gundry, *The Use of the Old Testament in St Matthew's Gospel* (1967).

prophet like one of the old prophets (Mk. 6: 15; 8: 28; Lk. 7: 16, 39) shows that His work must have appeared like that of a prophet to them. Jesus' use of the proverbial phrase, "No prophet is acceptable in his own country" (Lk. 4: 24) shows that He did not regard the title of prophet as an inappropriate one. Indeed, He clearly laid claim to the title, and could represent His fate as being simply what an unpopular prophet might expect (Lk. 13: 33).

What was the origin of this concept of Jesus' person and work? In Dt. 18: 15, 18 there is a promise from God through Moses: "The Lord your God will raise up for you a prophet like me from among you, from your brethren – him you shall heed . . . I will raise up for them a prophet like you from among their brethren; and I will put my words in his mouth, and he shall speak to them all that I command him." In its original context this promise refers to God's raising up of prophets from time to time to deliver His word to His people; a contrast is drawn with false prophets who may appear alongside them and with whom they may be confused. But by the time of Jesus there had grown up an expectation of one prophet *par excellence* who would be God's last messenger to His people. When the people asked John the Baptist, "Are you *the* prophet?" (Jn. 1: 21, 25), this was what they had in mind, and more than once the question was raised whether Jesus Himself was this prophet (Lk. 7: 39 RV mg; Jn. 6: 14; 7: 40). There is some evidence that Jesus may have regarded Himself as a second Moses, especially as He is presented in the Gospel of Matthew as the giver of a new law, and the point was explicitly made by Peter when he described Jesus in words drawn from Dt. 18 in his sermon after the healing of the lame man in the temple (Acts 3: 22 f.).[8]

Alongside Moses another Old Testament figure must be mentioned in this connection. Among the greatest of the prophets stood Elijah, and the Jews expected that Elijah would return, or that another 'Elijah' would come before the end of the world as God's herald. The promise expressed in Mal. 4: 5, "Behold, I will send you Elijah the prophet before the great and terrible day of the Lord comes", was taken up by the Jews, and one of the suggestions made about Jesus was that He was Elijah (Mk. 6: 15; 8: 28). One may find certain similarities between the work of Elijah and that of Jesus (Lk. 4: 25 f.), but there was a definite difference between them also

[8]There is a judicious discussion in W. D. Davies, *The Setting of the Sermon on the Mount* (1964), pp. 14–108.

(Lk. 9: 54 f. with RSV mg). Jesus Himself said who the second 'Elijah' was, namely John the Baptist (Mt. 17: 13; Mk. 9: 13). Even if John himself humbly dissociated himself from this role (Jn. 1: 21), yet he did go before the Lord 'in the spirit and the power of Elijah' (Lk. 1: 17).

It is possible to explain much of the work of Jesus in terms of His being a prophet. Indeed this might have been a sufficient designation of His role if He had been simply a mortal man; the travellers on the road to Emmaus had "hoped that he was the one to redeem Israel" (Lk. 24: 21), but as long as they knew only of His death they were forced to conclude that He was simply "Jesus of Nazareth, who was a prophet mighty in deed and word before God and all the people" (Lk. 24: 19). It needed the appearance of the risen Jesus to confirm their drooping faith and to lead them to the recognition that His claims to be more than a prophet were true.

Jesus the Son of Man

We shall find a more adequate description of Jesus in His own favourite self-designation as the Son of man. This is a Hebrew or Aramaic phrase which simply means 'man' in the sense of 'mankind' (the so-called 'generic' use) or 'the man' as a specific individual. The phrase is used in poetic parallelism with 'man' in Ps. 8: 4: "What is man that thou art mindful of him, and the son of man that thou dost' care for him?" (cf. Nu. 23: 19). From this quotation it appears that to some extent the phrase expresses the creatureliness and weakness of man over against his Creator. Nevertheless, it is this 'son of man' who has been made a little less than God and crowned with glory and honour (Ps. 8: 5). Hence the phrase could be used to describe Israel itself, as a people made strong by God (Ps. 80: 17), and it occurs frequently in Ezekiel as the name by which God addressed the prophet (e.g. Ezk. 2: 1). Most important is the way in which in Ezk. 1: 26 the One who sat 'above the likeness of a throne' is described as 'a likeness as it were of a human form'.[9] Here the phrase 'the son of man' is not used, but it seems likely that there is here a parallel to the famous description in Dn. 7: 13 f.: "Behold, with the clouds of heaven there came one like a son of man, and he came to

[9]On Elijah in the New Testament see J. Jeremias in *Theological Dictionary of the New Testament*, II, pp. 928–941.

the Ancient of Days and was presented before him. And to him was given dominion and glory and kingdom, that all peoples, nations and languages should serve him; his dominion is an everlasting dominion, which shall not pass away, and his kingdom one that shall not be destroyed." Two important facts emerge here. The first is that the figure like a son of man (i.e. like a man) is a heavenly being. The second is that in the interpretation of the vision the 'one like a son of man' is replaced by 'the saints of the Most High' (Dn. 7: 18, 25–27) who are the faithful people of Israel. It is possible that the 'one like a son of man' is simply a symbol for the saints of the Most High, just as Britannia is merely a symbol for the British people, but it is much more likely that he is their representative or head, just as a President or Prime Minister can be said to represent the people over whom he rules.

No further reference to this mysterious figure is found in the Old Testament, but in Jewish literature we find that the Son of man is the ruler who judges the world at the end of time and acts as God's representative (1 Enoch 69: 26–28). The dating of 1 Enoch is uncertain, but it is likely that in some Jewish circles during the time of Jesus the prophecy in Daniel remained alive. At the end of the age a heavenly figure like a man would appear to act as the judge and ruler appointed by God.

In the Gospels this title occurs about forty times in all, always as a self-designation of Jesus (Jn. 12: 34 is only an apparent exception). He used it in what we may call the traditional sense when He spoke of the coming of the Son of man in power and glory at the end of the age (Mk. 8: 38; 13: 26; 14: 62; Lk. 12: 8; 18: 8). But alongside this use there appears also a new sense of the title. It refers to Jesus as One who exercises divine authority on the earth, often in conditions of weakness and humiliation (Mk. 2: 10, 28; Mt. 8: 20; 11: 19); in particular Jesus used this title when He spoke of His suffering, rejection and resurrection (Mk. 8: 31; 14: 21, 41; et al.). This new use of the title is not clearly foreshadowed in the Old Testament (perhaps in Dn. 7: 21, 25), and we shall have to look more widely for an explanation of it.[10]

[10]Possibly no aspect of the teaching of Jesus has been the subject of such extensive discussion as has recently surrounded His use of this title. A survey of the most important recent literature up to 1965 is given in I. H. Marshall, 'The Synoptic Son of Man Sayings in Recent Discussion', *New Testament Studies* 12 (1965–66), pp. 327–351.

Jesus the Messiah

Before we answer this problem, however, we must observe the
curious fact that Jesus evidently preferred to think of Himself as the
Son of man rather than as the Messiah. This is all the more curious
when we recollect that Jesus' followers scarcely ever used this title
for Him (the exception is Acts 7: 56; cf. Rev. 1: 13; 14: 14) and that
'Christ' (the Greek translation of Messiah) became His name. How is
this to be explained?

'Messiah' is a word that means 'anointed', and it does not occur as
a title in the Old Testament. An anointed person might be a prophet,
priest or king, but only the anointed king was of real importance in
Jewish expectation. In the Old Testament there was to be found the
divine promise that God would set up a new king from the house of
David who would rule His people in justice and in freedom from
their enemies. This hope became stronger in the inter-testamental
period, especially when the people were oppressed by external foes
or disillusioned by their unworthy rulers, and they looked forward
to the coming of a king, anointed and appointed by God to deliver
them from their earthly oppressors.

When Jesus died on the cross, it was as a pretender to the Jewish
throne – "This is the king of the Jews" (Lk. 23: 38). The title, however, was one that He Himself had rarely claimed. He did accept the
affirmation of Peter that He was the Messiah, but He promptly told
His disciples to keep the matter quiet (Mk. 8: 29–30). Only at His
trial did He openly admit to being the Messiah (Mk. 14: 61–62).
Though conscious of being the Messiah, Jesus kept His identity
hidden from all except His most intimate companions for fear of
being misunderstood and misinterpreted. That this was no idle fear
is shown by the way in which the Jewish authorities had Jesus put
to death as soon as they felt that they had sufficient evidence that He
claimed to be, or was thought to be, the Messiah. The title of Messiah,
however distinguished its lineage, had become so debased in popular
expectation that Jesus could not safely use it. The Jews, like Pilate,
could not understand a kingship that was not of this world (Jn.
18: 36). In two ways the title of Son of man was better adapted to
Jesus' purposes. First, it included within itself all that was essential
in the title of Messiah, but, whereas the Messiah was simply an
earthly figure, the Son of man was a heavenly figure and the title
Son of man was a more appropriate one for the Son of God. Second,

the title Son of man was not current coinage in the same way as that of Messiah. Jesus had more freedom to fill it with new content. Further, it looks as though Jesus' usage of it was distinctly ambiguous; in certain of His sayings it may not have beeen clear that He was referring to Himself (Lk. 12: 8) or that He was in fact using a title at all (the phrase could simply mean 'man' as well as being a title). Jesus could, therefore, accomplish His work incognito, giving people the opportunity to decide for themselves what His work showed Him to be.

Jesus the Servant of the Lord

We may now return to Jesus' new concept of the Son of man as one whose authority is rejected and who suffers death. It is probable that several strands of thought should be distinguished in this idea. We should not forget that Jesus saw His fate in terms of that of the righteous man who suffers persecution on account of his faith in God (Pss. 22, 69; Wisdom 2–3). But of greatest importance is the figure of the Servant of the Lord described in the second part of the Book of Isaiah (Is. 40–55). The servant is appointed by God to establish justice in the earth, to bring Israel back to God, and to be a light to the nations so that salvation may extend to the end of the earth (Is. 42: 1–9). But the servant's reception by men includes insult and injury (Is. 49: 7; 50: 6), and ultimately he suffers death and dereliction. Yet he is mysteriously vindicated by God, and somehow death is not his final end (Is. 52: 13–53: 12).

The servant described in this prophecy is at times a collective figure for the people of Israel (Is. 44: 1), but the prophet saw that Israel was unfit for the task to which God called her (Is. 42: 18–25; 43: 22–28). Moreover, in some of the passages the description appears to be of an individual rather than of a group. It is, therefore, fairly commonly held that there was an oscillation in the prophet's mind between the people of Israel and a particular individual who would succeed where they had failed. Although there has been much questioning whether the prophet had some particular individual in mind, there was certainly only one person who can be said to have fulfilled the prophecy, Jesus Himself. The early church undoubtedly made the identification (Acts 8: 32–35; 1 Pet. 2: 21–25), and the Evangelists did likewise; it is sufficient to refer to the full quotation of Is. 42: 1–4 in Mt. 12: 17–21, where the healing miracles of Jesus are seen as a fulfilment of the hopes associated with the coming of the Servant of the Lord. Although it has sometimes been denied, there can be no doubt that Jesus Himself felt called to do the work of the Servant. We have already seen that He applied Is. 53: 12 to Himself (Lk. 22: 37), and to the evidence of that verse we may add Mk. 10: 45 and 14: 24 which allude to the same chapter in Isaiah.[11]

It is in this concept of humble service that we find the secret of the work of Jesus. Nowhere in the Old Testament is it said that the Messiah must suffer. Jesus realized that the One who was both Son of man and the Servant of the Lord must tread a path that was completely unfamiliar to His contemporaries. Authority and humility were paradoxically joined; acceptance by God and rejection by men went hand in hand. The One who came as God's last messenger to men was for the most part unrecognized.

The Teaching of Jesus

We have now gained what we may call a functional understanding of the person of Jesus. We have been concerned to examine not so much His personal relationship with the Father and the ontological character of His person as rather the particular roles which were for Him the concrete expression of the divine purpose which He came to fulfil. Our task is now to consider the outworking of these roles in the actual work of Jesus as prophet, Son of man and Servant of the Lord.

No one who reads the Gospels can fail to observe that there is an enormous amount of direct speech in them. A very large proportion of their content is made up of discourses by Jesus and dialogues in which He is the central figure. Even the stories which appear at first sight to recount His deeds were very often told more for the sake of the sayings of Jesus which they contain than because of the acts which they record. This is especially clear in John, where a mighty act performed by Jesus often becomes the starting-point (the modern jargon would be 'launching-pad') for an extended discourse in which

[11]The importance of the Servant concept for Jesus has been played down by M. D. Hooker, *Jesus and the Servant* (1959), but is convincingly defended by J. Jeremias (and W. Zimmerli) in *Theological Dictionary of the New Testament*, V, pp. 654–717. For the 'righteous man' see E. Schweizer, *Lordship and Discipleship* (1960), and for an attempt to find a *suffering* Son of Man in Daniel see C. K. Barrett, *Jesus and the Gospel Tradition* (1967).

its significance is elaborated. We shall not be far wrong if we look at the work of Jesus in the first instance as that of a prophet, a preacher and a teacher. The Gospels in fact make this explicit. Mark's opening summary of the work of Jesus tells us that He came into Galilee "preaching the gospel of God" (Mk. 1: 14). This is confirmed by the very similar account in Matthew (4: 17), and by the way in which Matthew presents Jesus as a teacher who gave comprehensive discourses to the people (Mt. 5–7, 10, 13, 18, 23–25; these discourses contain collections of sayings of Jesus spoken on several occasions). Likewise, Luke has put at the head of his Gospel a scene in the synagogue at Nazareth where Jesus announces that He has been commissioned to preach (Lk. 4: 15–19).

The Gospels use a variety of words to describe this activity of Jesus. They refer to it indifferently as 'preaching' or 'teaching'. Some theologians prefer to describe proclamation to the unconverted as 'preaching' and instruction of the converted as 'teaching', and the corresponding Greek nouns, *kerugma* (or *kerygma*) and *didache* have almost become technical terms for these activities. Convenient though this terminology may be, such a rigid distinction is not to be found in the Gospels; the non-believer needs to be instructed in the teaching of Jesus, and the believer needs to hear the challenging tones of the preaching of Jesus.[12] One other word which should be mentioned here is the verb 'to preach the gospel' (Gk. *euaggelizomai*) which indicates that the message of Jesus had a positive content.

The hearers of Jesus no doubt thought of Him as being like one of their religious teachers or rabbis. He gave discourses in the synagogues and sat to teach just like a rabbi, and this title of respect and similar ones, such as 'teacher', were addressed to Him by the people. Yet the character of what He said and the authority with which He said it (Mk. 1: 22) showed that He was no mere rabbi. In fact He had never received a rabbinic training (Jn. 7: 15). It was more appropriate to think of Him as a prophet, but we should not forget that one of the functions of the Servant of the Lord was to teach the people (Is. 50: 4; cf. 61: 1 f.).

The fact that Jesus is presented in the Gospels as a teacher should not mislead us into thinking that His words were necessarily the most significant part of His activity. It is better to think of Him as

[12]See J. J. Vincent, 'Didactic Kerygma in the Synoptic Gospels,' *Scottish Journal of Theology* 10 (1957), pp. 262–273.

the bringer of the gospel and to remember that the gospel needs more than words to bring it to men. We must not make an artificial distinction between the words of Jesus and His deeds, the mighty works that surprised the people and the acts of love and compassion which made the gospel a reality to them. Moreover, when the first Christians looked back to the work of Jesus, the thing that formed the centre of their preaching was not what He taught but the fact that He had died and been resurrected. Word and deed belong insepably together; Jesus came, it has been said, not so much to preach the gospel as that there might be a gospel to preach. It is, however, to the words of Jesus that we must look for the significance of what He did.

The Kingdom of God

The main theme of the teaching and ministry of Jesus was the kingdom of God.[18] The kingdom, or rather the kingship, of God is the correlative of the Messiah as the future ruler appointed by God. Although the Old Testament bore ample witness to the fact that God, the creator of heaven and earth, is their present ruler, the writers were conscious that His kingly power was far from being universally recognized and obeyed. His own people suffered much from human oppression, and they eagerly received the message of the prophets that at some time in the future God would act in kingly power to save His people from their enemies and to set up an era of peace and righteousness. Sometimes this future kingdom was regarded as being set up under the messianic king of the house of David; at other times the Messiah is passed over in silence, and all the emphasis is on the kingly rule of God Himself. The hymn of Zechariah at the birth of his son is an excellent example of the character of this hope and at the same time testifies to the living quality of this hope among Jews at the time of the birth of Jesus. The past tenses are a characteristic Jewish way of referring to future events conceived as already taking place: "Blessed be the Lord God of Israel, for he has visited and redeemed his people, and has raised up

___

[18]The alternative form of the title, 'the kingdom of heaven', is synonymous, and owes its origin to the frequent Jewish avoidance of the actual name of God in their speech and writing. On the kingdom generally see R. Schnackenburg, *God's Rule and Kingdom* (1963); G. E. Ladd, *Jesus and the Kingdom* (1966).

a horn of salvation for us in the house of his servant David, as he spoke by the mouth of his holy prophets from of old . . . that we, being delivered from the hand of our enemies, might serve him without fear, in holiness and righteousness before him all the days of our life" (Lk. 1: 68–70, 74–75).

It was in the context of such expectation that Jesus announced that the kingly rule of God was about to begin: "The time is fulfilled, and the kingdom of God is at hand; repent and believe the good news" (Mk. 1: 15). Like a prophet of old He announced that God was about to act, and to act soon.

But the message of Jesus was so different from popular expectations that it was not universally accepted. The Jewish hope was intensely nationalistic. The people thought of the kingdom of God in terms of a successful political revolution against the Romans which would remove them from the seats of power and reduce them to underdogs and slaves. There was nothing of this in the message of Jesus. In His preaching He significantly omitted reference to the vengeance of God upon the Gentiles (cf. Lk. 4: 19 with its source in Is. 61: 2), and He obviously had no thought of being the leader of a political revolution: witness His repudiation of the implied suggestion that tribute should not be paid to Rome (Mk. 12: 13–17) and His refusal to assume a kingly role when it was offered to Him (Jn. 6: 15). On the contrary, His teaching was about a spiritual rule of God – but a spiritual rule that had a great deal to do with the world of politics and power (e.g. Mk. 10: 42–45). The real opposition to the rule of God came not from an oppressive set of overlords but from the supernatural forces of evil and the demonic powers which controlled the hearts of all men, both Roman and Jewish.

Moreover, Jesus went beyond Jewish expectations by announcing that the rule of God was already present. There is a certain tension in His statements between assertions that the kingdom had already come and that it was soon to come in the future. We must think of the kingdom coming, as it were, in stages. It came quietly and almost unrecognized in the ministry of Jesus, but He looked forward to its glorious, open manifestation and consummation in the future.

This brings us to a point of supreme importance. There had been prophets before Jesus who had announced that God would shortly act in power. John the Baptist, the contemporary of Jesus, preached the same message (cf. Mt. 3: 2). But Jesus was more than such a prophet. He came as God's agent to establish His rule. It is no exag-

geration to say that His ministry *was* the kingdom of God. He was
the Messiah, and His coming was the coming of the rule of God. We
can now consider His work more closely.

The Revealer of God

We have already observed that the deepest truth about the person of
Jesus in the New Testament is that He is the Son of God. The con-
verse is also true, namely that the character of God is that He is the
Father.

Now the fact that God is the Father of His people was by no
means new when Jesus taught it. The Old Testament bears abundant
witness that God cares for His people as a father does for his children.
The Jews in the time of Jesus had inherited this belief. They had
rightly perceived that God is not the Father of each and every man,
but only of those with whom He has entered into a covenant and
whom He has chosen as His people, men who for their part give Him
the faith and obedience that a father should receive. Nowhere does
the Bible support the popular heresy that God is the Father of all
men. But for many Jews God remained somewhat remote, and it
tended to be assumed that acceptance by Him depended upon a man's
achievement of a high standard of piety and righteousness.

The new thing in the teaching of Jesus was that He admitted all
men to the same intimate relationship with God which He uniquely
possessed by nature, and He offered this privilege to them, irrespec-
tive of the quality of their past lives, if they became His disciples.
When Jesus spoke to God in prayer, He addressed Him by the
Aramaic word *Abba*, 'Father', which was the intimate form of
address that a child would use to its earthly father and not the
formal word customarily used in prayer (Mk. 14:36); it has been
conclusively shown that in this respect the prayers of Jesus were
unique in Judaism.[14] What is significant is that Jesus taught His
disciples to pray to God using this same word (Mt. 6: 9; Lk. 11: 2),
and they were so conscious of the unprecedented character of this
prayer that years after His death even Greek-speaking Christians
continued to use this same Aramaic word in their prayers (Rom. 8:
15; Gal. 4: 6). In this way Jesus revealed God to His disciples as a
Father to whom they could pray as intimately as He could.
God was indeed now His Father and their Father, His God and

[14]J. Jeremias, *The Central Message of the New Testament* (1965), ch. 1.

their God (Jn. 20: 17), a form of speech which both preserves the distinction between the One who is Son by nature and those who are sons by grace, and puts them all into the same relationship with God.

In the same way, Jesus taught His disciples to put their trust in a heavenly Father who cares deeply for them and who wishes to free them from all worry and needless anxiety (Mt. 6: 25–34; Lk. 12: 22–34). It is this aspect of the teaching of Jesus which has struck many by its freshness and simplicity and especially by its lack of dogma and complicated doctrine. Here, they have said, is the essence of the religion of Jesus, a simple, unencumbered faith in the fatherly goodness of God which will carry men through every vicissitude of life. The point is true enough, so far as it goes; what must not be forgotten is that this teaching about the nature of God formed part of the teaching of Jesus about the kingship of God. "The King in the Kingdom is a Father", as A. M. Hunter put it.[15] But the Father is also the King, and His fatherly goodness is revealed only to those who accept Him as their King.

The teaching of Jesus thus reveals the character of God. But Jesus also revealed God by acting as God acts and in His name. When He raised the son of the widow at Nain to life, the bystanders glorified God and said, "A great prophet has arisen among us" and "God has visited his people" (Lk. 7: 16). The expressions show that they did not identify Jesus with God, but they did perceive clearly that God was working in and through Him. Further evidence was available for them in the way in which Jesus acted with divine authority. For example, He forgave sins. Admittedly a prophet could pronounce forgiveness in the name of God (2 Sam. 12: 13), but Jesus did so as the Son of man, as God's representative empowered to act on earth on His behalf (Mk. 2: 10). Likewise, He claimed authority as Lord of the sabbath, thus asserting that He had jurisdiction over what is pre-eminently the *Lord's* day (Mk. 2: 28). Finally, looking to the future, Jesus claimed divine authority to act as judge at the last day (Mk. 8: 38; 14: 62; Lk. 12: 25–27), and He made it clear that a divine judgement was already in progress; the attitude of men to Him in this life would determine their fate on the last day.

Throughout the ministry of Jesus this note of supreme authority is sounded. One of His most characteristic forms of utterance was to

[15]*Introducing New Testament Theology* (1957), p. 31.

preface a statement with the word 'verily' or 'truly' (Gk. *amen*). The word is one of confirmation and attestation. Normally it was used to confirm what somebody else said. Only Jesus dared to use it of His own statements; speaking with the authority of God, He required nobody else to confirm the truth of what He said. In this single word, one eminent scholar has stated, "we have the whole of Christology *in nuce*".[16]

The underlying basis of this authority is laid bare in the Gospel of John. As the Son who was obedient to His Father, and as the Son of man sent by God into the world, Jesus had received the authority to bestow *life* upon men and to execute *judgement*. (Jn. 5: 19–29). These two activities, which between them sum up the work of Jesus, are, however, exclusively divine activities. Jesus' authority derived from the fact that God had commissioned Him to act with His own authority in the world as Saviour and Judge of men.

It was, however, not simply divine authority that was seen in Jesus. The love and compassion of the heavenly Father accompanied the authority of the King. When Jesus offered forgiveness to the sinful, He did so in God's name. He demonstrated the grace of the Father who welcomes the prodigal son home without asking him any embarrassing questions and who overwhelms him with his love. He spoke words of grace and pardon to those who had fallen so low in human estimation that it required divine love to reach them and lift them from their plight. (Lk. 7: 36–50). The accusation, "Behold, a glutton and a drunkard, a friend of tax collectors and sinners" (Mt. 11: 19) concealed the truth that in Jesus the love of God was supremely revealed. And when Jesus attempted to reply to such accusations, the way in which He did so was by telling parables which echoed, however faintly, the joy which is felt in heaven at the repentance and home coming of sinners (Lk. 15: 7, 10).

All this puts us in the position to appreciate the words of Jesus in Mt. 11: 25–27 (Lk. 10: 21–22) in which He claims the unique privilege of revealing the Father to men.[17] His work was to reveal God. If a person wishes to see what God is like, the traditional Christian answer has always been, "Look at Jesus". To say this is simply to

[16]H. Schlier in *Theological Dictionary of the New Testament*, I, p. 338.
[17]We may note in passing that the description of the work of Jesus which we have offered above demonstrates how apposite is the summary of that work in this text, and goes a long way towards neutralizing the objections often raised against the authenticity of this utterance.

repeat the conversation between Jesus and Philip: "Lord, show us the Father, and we shall be satisfied." "He who has seen me has seen the Father" (Jn. 14: 8–9). The man who has seen Jesus does not need to look any further.

The Conqueror of Satan

We have just been considering the work of Jesus from the so-called *doxological* point of view, and have seen that He revealed God the King as a Father to men. It may be useful now to take up the *antagonistic* motif, and consider the work of Jesus in relation to the devil.

A type of theology, now well and truly laid to rest, used to think of the ministry of Jesus as "a peaceful pastoral wherein the serene wisdom of the Teacher accorded well with the flowers and birds of Galilee". Such an idyllic view makes nonsense of the Gospels. "The emergent picture of the Chief Figure in the campaign," writes A. M. Hunter, "so far from being that of a high-souled teacher patiently indoctrinating the multitudes with truths of timeless wisdom, is rather that of the strong Son of God, armed with his Father's power, spear-heading the attack against the devil and all his works, and calling men to decide on whose side of the battle they will be."[18]

The evidence is ready to hand. In acting as the bringer of the kingdom of God, Jesus placed Himself in total opposition to the kingdom of Satan. He was the one who claimed to have the kingdoms of the world at his disposal (Lk. 4: 6), and men and women held in the grip of suffering were said by Jesus to be under his sway (Lk. 13: 16; probably also Mk. 7: 35). The task of Jesus was to dethrone "the prince of this world" (Jn. 12: 31).

In a vivid parable Jesus told how it is impossible to plunder a strong man's house without first rendering the owner powerless (Mk. 3: 27). The context shows that He was thinking of His own work of overcoming Satan and setting his captives free. So far was Jesus from being in league with Satan, as His enemies alleged (Mk. 3: 22), that He was engaged in a fight to the finish with him. He claimed to be the Stronger One who had power to bind Satan and release his prisoners (Lk. 11: 22), and He gave authority to His disciples to carry on the campaign (Lk. 10: 19). If we take the saying of Jesus literally, the

[18]*Introducing New Testament Theology*, pp. 17 and 18.

implication would be that He had 'bound' Satan at the beginning of His ministry, no doubt in the wilderness conflict (Mt. 4: 1–11).[19] The objection to this view, namely that Satan was still very active after his initial defeat, is not a strong one, for Satan remained active even after the victory of Easter. Nevertheless, it may be wise not to take the saying too literally and to see in it simply a declaration of the superior might of Jesus which enabled Him to set Satan's victims at liberty.

From this point of view the whole of the ministry of Jesus was a campaign against Satanic power. It began with Satan's attack upon Jesus personally. It concluded with the death and exaltation of Jesus, which He declared prophetically to be the moment of Satan's defeat and dethronement (Jn. 12: 31). The intervening period was, perhaps less obviously, a conflict with the powers of darkness. This was certainly true of the activity of Jesus in expelling demons from the men and women whom they had held in evil bondage. Whatever view we may take of the meaning of demon possession, there is no doubt that it expressed the reality of the superhuman power of evil that can hold men in its sway and from which only a spiritual salvation can give release. A point of particular interest is the observation that the language used to describe the relations of Jesus with human opponents is very similar to that used of His relations with demonic opponents. When the Pharisees came and asked Jesus for a sign, their action is described as 'tempting him' (Mk. 8: 11). Even Peter could take on the role of Satan when he tried to dissuade Jesus from His appointed path (Mk. 8: 33). In the last analysis, all evil has the same origin and character.

Two extremes must be avoided in examining the work of Jesus from this aspect. On the one hand, the extent of satanic activity may be minimized. For example, it has been argued on the basis of Luke 4: 13 and 22: 3 that the actual period of the ministry of Jesus between these points was free from satanic influence.[20] But although references to Satan himself are rare during the ministry of Jesus, the point is rather a forced one. The opposition to Jesus did not come directly from Satan, but it was hardly necessary to name him every time that men or demons motivated by evil took the field against Jesus.

[19]So E. Best, *The Temptation and the Passion* (1965), p. 13.
[20]H. Conzelmann, *The Theology of St Luke* (1960), p. 28; E. Best, *The Temptation and the Passion* (1965).

On the other hand, we should guard against reading the activity of Satan into the story at every point. By so doing, one might conclude that the cross of Jesus was basically a place of conflict with Satan in which he was defeated. Such is undoubtedly an important part of the meaning of the cross, and we owe a debt to those scholars who have reminded us of a neglected area of theology.[21] Nevertheless, as Dr E. Best has shown, it is far from being central in the Gospels, and in order to understand the significance of the cross we must considerably widen our perspective.

The Saviour of Men

Up to this point we have spoken of the work of Jesus in terms of His association with the kingdom of God. But there is an important aspect of the work of Jesus which is not readily conveyed to our modern ears by the use of this phrase, and therefore we must now bring into consideration another word, frequently found in the Gospels, which expresses this point. The word *salvation* expresses the vital fact that the exercise of God's kingship in the last days means His action to save and redeem His people.[22] Thus when Simeon saw the young child Jesus in the temple, he was able to say to God, "Mine eyes have seen thy salvation" (Lk. 2: 30). As the angel indicated to Joseph, the child's name was to be 'Jesus' (a common enough Jewish name, equivalent to the Old Testament form 'Joshua'), which means 'Saviour', because this indicated the work that He was to do (Mt. 1: 21). Jesus' own consciousness that this was to be His task is summed up in His words in the house of Zacchaeus: "Today salvation has come to this house . . . for the Son of man came to seek and to save the lost" (Lk. 19: 9 f.).

The Mighty Works of Jesus

As the Saviour of men Jesus brought to them the blessings associated with the reign of God. His mighty acts of healing were signs on the physical level of the presence of salvation. The era of fulfilment had come (Mt. 11: 2–6), and the disciples of Jesus were privileged to behold it (Lk. 10; 23–24).

The mighty acts of healing performed by Jesus appeared to the

[21]G. Aulén, *Christus Victor* (1931); R. Lelvestad, *Christ the Conqueror* (1964).
[22]E. M. B. Green, *The Meaning of Salvation* (1965).

a

people to be miraculous. They were not performed by a purely human power but as a result of divine power working specially and directly through Jesus. It is possible that a modern observer might be able to interpret some, though certainly not all, of the healings and exorcisms performed by Jesus in a more 'natural' manner. We now know sufficient about psycho-somatic illness, for example, to understand that certain forms of paralysis may be cured by removing the psychological trouble which has expressed itself in this physical manner; it may well be that the new mental health which Jesus brought to men and women contributed to their physical healing. To say this is not to rationalize the miracles or to deny the fact of divine power manifested in them. The point is rather this: whereas we tend to see the significance of the mighty works of Jesus in their supernatural, miraculous character, this is probably not their real importance. Their real significance is that the presence of Jesus brought health and cleansing to the needy, and demonstrated that the era of salvation had come. Whether the signs were worked by Jesus through natural or supernatural power in each instance is secondary to the fact that men and women actually experienced the healing power of God and were able to live life again as God intended it to be lived.

This explains why the Pharisees and the multitudes could ask Jesus for a sign even after He had just performed so remarkable a work as the feeding of the five thousand (Mk. 8: 11; Jn. 6: 30). Plenty of remarkable incidents attributed rightly or wrongly to supernatural power took place in the ancient world. What the opponents of Jesus wanted was clear evidence that He was commissioned by God; it was a sign *from heaven* that they wanted rather than a conjuring trick that could equally well have been inspired by Satan (cf. Mt. 12: 24, 27). Jesus certainly did perform such mighty acts, which ought to have been sufficient proof that the kingdom of God had really come (Mt. 12: 28), but He was loth to provide demonstrations of power to order. His purpose was not to compel men to believe through impressive feats of divine power which would overawe them. Such belief is worth nothing; it involves no moral and spiritual change of heart on the part of the observers. They will simply be like people who obey the policeman only because they have reason to fear his authority; take away his authority, and they will treat him with contempt.

The mighty works of Jesus show that He regarded the physical well-being of men as one of the blessings of God's salvation. We have seen earlier that He taught His followers about the fatherly care of God which sets men free from worry about material affairs. To say this is not to deny the supremacy of the spiritual. It is rather to enter a plea that the physical and the material must not be forgotten. We dare not forget or explain away the fact of Jesus' concern for the well-being of the whole man in the interests of some higher spirituality. There is indeed a case for a 'spiritual' interpretation of the miracles of Jesus; leprosy may be regarded as an illustration of sin, and Jesus Himself may well have regarded His cures of the blind and the deaf as symbols of the spiritual illumination which He gave to His disciples. Preachers would be much the poorer if they did not believe it right to use the miracle stories in this way. But over against this view it must be emphasized that the *primary* purpose of the healing miracles was to *heal* the physically and mentally afflicted. Salvation cannot be limited to one aspect of human need, for the whole man is the object of divine concern. Christians must ask very seriously what are the implications of the healing ministry of Jesus for the church today.

Jesus and Human Sin

On the spiritual level, the work of Jesus largely consisted of teaching and exhortation. Men were urged to accept the good news that Jesus had come to establish the kingdom of God and to repent and put their faith in Jesus. At first sight, it might seem that Jesus was concerned with an intellectual need on the part of men. What they needed was illumination and instruction, so that they might see the true state of affairs and then make their response. We recollect that the teaching of Jesus contains numerous references to blindness and lack of understanding. The Pharisees were castigated more than once for their failure to appreciate the message of Jesus and for their lack of moral and spiritual perception into the word of God in the Old Testament (Mt. 15: 12–14; 23: 16–26; Jn. 9: 39–41). Even the disciples of Jesus frequently failed to understand His message and had to be rebuked by Him (Mt. 15: 15 f.; Mk. 8: 14–21, 32 f.; 9: 32). To describe their condition Jesus used a word which means 'hardness' or 'blindness' of heart (Mk. 3: 5; 6: 52; 8: 17; Jn. 12: 40). The things that Jesus said and did were like riddles to them (Mk. 4: 11–12; the word 'parable' can have the meaning of 'riddle').

We might perhaps think of the puzzle picture that appears in books for children. The picture appears to contain simply, let us say, the branches and leaves of a tree, but when a person looks more carefully he sees that the artist has cunningly contrived some of the details so that there is a human face lurking among the branches. So the words and deeds of Jesus appeared as ordinary, human deeds to men; it required insight to perceive that they had a deeper, divine significance and that in these acts the saving power and love of God were revealed.

But was the failure of Jesus' contemporaries purely an intellectual one? A person may not be able to discover for himself the face hidden in the puzzle picture but still have sufficient ability to see it when somebody else points it out to him. But there is a difference between that kind of puzzle and the test used to determine colour blindness. In such a test the subject is shown a picture made up of coloured dots. A person with normal vision sees a background of one colour with a symbol (e.g. a letter of the alphabet) inscribed on it in another colour. The colour-blind person who by nature cannot distinguish between the two colours used for the symbol and the background sees only one uniform colour, and no matter how carefully somebody else explains the picture to him he will never be able to 'see' it. It is not more intelligence he needs, but new eyes. What was wrong with the people who heard and saw Jesus was not an intellectual lack but a blindness of heart that required a more radical cure.

The people in fact suffered from the blindness caused by sin. Despite much that is popularly believed about Jesus' conviction of the essential goodness of men, the inescapable fact is that He taught as stern a doctrine of sin as is to be found anywhere in the Bible.[23] They were rebels against God, captives under the sway of evil. Nothing that they could do was able to set them free. One might have thought that an attractive young man, like the rich ruler who faithfully tried to keep all the commandments and longed for eternal life, would easily have been won over from the love of wealth which was his particular temptation, but Jesus sadly commented, "It is easier for a camel to go through the eye of a needle than for a rich man to enter the kingdom of God." And when the disciples asked in wonder, "Then who can be saved?" Jesus replied, "With men it is impossible" (Mk. 10: 25–27). It is only when a person is converted

[23]W. G. Kümmel, *Man in the New Testament* (1962).

and undergoes a transformation of his nature that entry to the king-dom becomes possible (Mt. 18: 3; Mk. 10: 15; Jn. 3: 3, 5). How that is possible is not explained in the teaching of Jesus; it is as mysterious as the motion of the wind (Jn. 3: 8). All we are told is that it is pos-sible with God (Mk. 10: 27), and beyond that we cannot go. From the human point of view, the Gospels simply show us that when men and women received the message of Jesus and became His disciples, the miracle was wrought in their hearts.

Jesus and the Church

The saving work of Jesus, therefore, consisted in His deeds and words through which the saving power of God was brought to men. The kingly might of God, rescuing men from evil and sin, was revealed in the ministry of Jesus. As the Son of God, His acts and His words were the vehicles of divine, saving might, so that those who responded to His word found that their faith had made them whole and that they were enjoying the blessings of the kingdom of God.

In this way we are brought to consider briefly the work of Jesus in relation to His followers. The essential response which He de-manded of men was that they should become His disciples. It is no accident that the brief summary of Jesus' message that men should repent and believe the gospel (Mk. 1: 15) is followed immediately by the story of four men who heard Jesus say, 'Follow me', and left all to become His disciples (Mk. 1: 16–20). Nothing could indicate more clearly that to accept the gospel of the kingdom means to accept Jesus Himself. His role, therefore, with regard to those who respond to the message which He proclaimed is that of 'Teacher and Lord' (Jn. 13: 13; cf. Mt. 23: 8–10). From this point of view, His work may be summarized, first, as that of providing an example. The supreme teacher is the one who embodies his teaching in his own life. Jesus showed this when He washed His disciples' feet and gave them to understand that this was an example of the humble service that they were to show to each other (Jn. 13: 1–20). The lesson was one that needed to be driven home often, as is evidenced by the fre-quency with which it recurs in the Gospels (Mk. 9: 35; 10: 42–44; Lk. 22: 24–27).

Jesus also appears as the teacher of the disciples. Although the word 'esoteric' has gained a bad meaning through being used of those

religious sects which purvey higher truths to an exclusive group of
élite members, it can be legitimately used with regard to Jesus to
remind us that those who are His disciples are admitted into a deeper
knowledge of God than is possible outside this group. T. W. Manson
aptly applied to the teaching of Jesus the words of Plato: "To find
the maker and father of this universe is a hard task; and when you
have found him, it is impossible to speak of him before all people"
(*Timaeus*, 28 c).[24] Jesus Himself voiced the same thought, "Do not
give dogs what is holy, and do not throw your pearls before swine"
(Mt. 7: 6). Spiritual teaching can be given only to the spiritually
minded (cf. 1 Cor. 2: 13 f.). Hence Jesus gave His more profound
teaching to His disciples, both for their own spiritual illumination
and in order to prepare them to carry on His task of mission to the
world (Mk. 3: 14). To them He revealed the truth of the Fatherhood
of God, and with them He shared the secrets of His own person and
work.

The disciples for their part accepted Jesus as their Master. The
nearest contemporary parallel was probably that of a group of
pupils gathered around a respected rabbi, but, as K. H. Rengstorf
has observed, He was more than a rabbi or teacher; He was the
Lord.[25] They gave Him their obedience (Lk. 6: 46–49), although they
often failed to understand Him and were to prove faithless in the
hour of trial (Mk. 14: 50).

Finally, Jesus was their Saviour in the sense that He cared for
them and promised to be with them (Mt. 18: 20). The picture which
Jesus especially used to bring out this aspect of His work was that
of the shepherd (Jn. 10: 1–30). He saw His disciples as a flock, liable
to meet danger and too weak in themselves to withstand it, and He
promised to them that they would be kept and preserved by the
Father and Himself (Lk. 12: 32). Admittedly, He did not promise
them freedom from tribulation and persecution; if the Shepherd
was to be smitten, the flock must also be prepared to suffer (Mk.
14: 27). But He did promise them His prayers in their hour of
need (Lk. 22: 31 f.), the help of the Spirit (Lk. 12: 11 f.) and the
assurance of entry into the heavenly kingdom of God. With His
last words He assured them of His presence with them (Mt. 28:
20).

[24] T. W. Manson, *The Teaching of Jesus* (1935²), pp. 90, 108.
[25] K. H. Rengstorf in *Theological Dictionary of the New Testament*, IV, p.
455.

The Death of Jesus

An attentive reader might well protest at this point that we have displayed a certain lack of proportion in our study. The number of disciples who gave their allegiance to Jesus was undoubtedly small. And the vast claims which He made to them were brought to a sudden end by His death. The nation as a whole rejected Him, and He came to His end on a gallows. We are bound to go back and consider what significance must be attached to the death of Jesus.

One factor that militates against the sceptical estimate of the work of Jesus which we have just expressed is that the Gospels make it quite clear that Jesus taught and worked as He did in the full consciousness that death and rejection by the people lay ahead of Him. The early church certainly considered the death of Jesus (and all that was associated with it) to be the chief part of His story; there are several indications that the story of the last week in Jesus' life, which occupies a quite disproportionate amount of space in all the Gospels, was the first part to be committed to writing as a connected narrative. And according to the Gospels, the turning-point in the work of Jesus came when, having elicited the fact that His disciples believed Him to be the Messiah, Jesus began to teach them that He must suffer (Mt. 16: 21). When Jesus adopted the role of the Servant of the Lord, He knew what lay ahead of Him. Jesus did not perform His messianic work despite the foreknowledge that He must die, but somehow saw it as the fitting climax of His work. How then did He view it?

One possible interpretation is that He saw death as a kind of occupational risk, the price that must be paid by a man who upsets the *status quo* too violently and stirs up too many vested interests. There were plenty of people before Jesus who had had to die for their beliefs. Jesus Himself spoke of the way in which Jerusalem slew the prophets. The precedent of earlier prophets made Him none too sanguine about His own chances when He left the comparative calm of Galilee for the capital city (Lk. 13: 33). Over the Gospels there looms the shadow of John the Baptist who had remained faithful to his message of righteousness to the point of imprisonment and death. Throughout His ministry, even in Galilee, Jesus had known what it was to be rejected and despised even by erstwhile friends (Mk. 6: 1–6; Lk. 4: 16–30; Jn. 6: 66); there had been groups of official inquirers who came to see what He was doing (Mk. 3: 22);

attempts had been made to trap Him (Mk. 3: 1–2) and even to arrest
Him (Jn. 7: 30–32), and there was continual plotting against His life
(Mk. 3: 6; Jn. 11: 53). Jesus was well aware of what was happening,
and yet He persisted on His course. And so in the end He perished
for His beliefs. 'The blood of the martyrs is the seed of the church'.
The courage of Jesus shows how passionately He believed in the
truth of His message; His moral integrity forbade Him to yield to the
opposition. He trusted in God to vindicate His cause and to deliver
Him (Mt. 27: 43).

And God did vindicate Him by raising Him from the dead. He
attested that Jesus was His Son and that His words were God's Word.
The message of Jesus was shown to be true; His work came to
fruition.

Jesus a martyr for His message. This interpretation of the death
of Jesus is both plausible and true. But it cannot be the whole truth,
for it fails to reckon with a whole chain of evidence that must now
be considered. There is first the strange insistence of Jesus that His
life was not taken from Him, but that He freely and voluntarily
gave it up (Mt. 26: 53; Jn. 10: 18). As the Son of God, He believed
that He did not need to die, and yet He chose to die.

There is that strange scene in the Garden of Gethsemane in which
Jesus prayed to His Father that the cup which He was about to drink
might be averted from Him (Mk. 14: 36). One may perhaps regard
this as the agonized cry of a man who is about to face martyrdom
but longs that the path of duty may not bring him to this point, but
this is a somewhat strained interpretation. It becomes strained to the
point of impossibility when we take the wording seriously and inquire into the associations of the word 'cup'. We find that the word
is used in contexts which speak of the wrath of God poured out for
men to drink. Jeremiah prophesied judgement upon the nations with
the words, "Thus the Lord, the God of Israel, said to me: 'Take from
my hand this cup of the wine of wrath, and make all the nations to
whom I send you drink it. They shall drink and stagger and be crazed
because of the sword which I am sending among them'" (Jer. 25:
15 f.; cf. Ps. 75: 8; Is. 51: 17–23; Ezk. 23: 31–34). L. Goppelt rightly
comments on the scene in Gethsemane, "The unspeakable grief and
fear which evokes the request that what lies ahead may be avoided
is not terror before a dark fate nor alarm in view of physical suffering and death but the dread of the One whose life depended upon
God at the thought of being cast away from God and of facing the

judgement in which the Holy One is delivered up to the power of sin."[26]

Moreover, this was not the first time that Jesus had spoken this way. Earlier He had spoken to His disciples of the cup which He must drink and the baptism which He must face (Mk. 10: 38 f.; Lk. 12: 50). The imagery of baptism likewise refers to undergoing suffering (cf. Ps. 42: 7; 69: 1 f.). Then, when He actually hung on the cross, He who had addressed God as Father even in Gethsemane cried, "My God, my God, why hast thou forsaken me?" (Mk. 15: 34).

These sayings of Jesus compel us to seek for some deeper explanation of His death than that it was simply the fate of a martyr. The answer to our question is not exactly proclaimed from the housetops in the Gospels. It has been said that it was difficult for Jesus to explain the significance of His death to the disciples when it was hard for them even to accept the simple fact that He was going to die. Consequently, the Gospels lay more stress on the necessity of the death of Jesus and on the fact that it was part of His destiny than upon its deeper meaning. The reader who comes to the passion story in the Gospels after a study of the Epistles cannot fail to be impressed by the lack of dogmatic elucidation; the stress is much more on the way in which the death of Jesus fulfilled Old Testament prophecy, and is no doubt to be seen as part of the early church's teaching to the Jews that a crucified man could be the Messiah. As we have seen, however, the Old Testament prophecy of which great use was made in this way was that of the suffering Servant of the Lord, and there is evidence that Jesus interpreted the meaning of His death from this area of the Old Testament.

Two passages lift the veil to some extent and allow us to see into the mind of Jesus. The first is the saying in Mark 10: 45: "For the Son of man also came not to be served but to serve, and to give his life as a ransom for many." The concluding words of this saying 'for many' are a fairly plain pointer to Is. 53: 10–12, where we read about the Servant: "He makes himself an offering for sin . . . By his knowledge shall the righteous one, my servant, make *many* to be accounted righteous; and he shall bear their iniquities . . . He poured out his soul to death, and was numbered with the transgressors; yet he bore the sin of *many*, and made intercession for the transgressors." It emerges that the death of Jesus was regarded as

[26]L. Goppelt in G. Kittel (ed.), *Theologisches Wörterbuch zum Neuen Testament* (1933–), VI, p. 153.

somehow conferring benefit upon 'the many'. His death was a means of bearing their sin and enabling them to be accounted righteous. A further Old Testament passage which strengthens this understanding of the words of Jesus is to be found in Psalm 49. In verses 7–9 the writer comments that no man is able to 'buy off' death: "Truly no man can ransom himself, or give to God the price of his life, for the ransom of his life is costly, and can never suffice, that he should continue to live on for ever, and never see the Pit." The thought is exactly the same as in Mk. 8: 36 f., "What can a man give in return for his life?" and confirms our belief that Jesus had the words of the Psalm in mind. The Psalm stresses the inevitability of death, although admittedly without drawing a direct connection with sin. But then it goes on to affirm that where man is powerless God can act: "But God will ransom my soul from the power of Sheol, for he will receive me " (Ps. 49: 15). The thought of God providing a ransom for the souls of men is what Jesus expresses. He is the ransom provided by God, for He bears death on behalf of the many that they may be redeemed from destruction. He acts as their substitute in doing for them what they could not do for themselves. He performs an act of universal significance, for it has been convincingly shown by J. Jeremias that 'many' is a Hebrew figure of speech for 'all'.[27]

The second saying of Jesus, which confirms our understanding of Mk. 10: 45, is to be found in His words at the last supper. At the passover meal it was customary for the roast lamb to be made the basis of an 'object lesson' about the significance of the supper and its historical basis in the slaying of the lambs to redeem the people when they departed from their captivity in Egypt. Jesus did not take up this symbolism (but see 1 Cor. 5: 7 for Paul's use of it), but used the bread and wine which formed part of the meal for a similar exposition. The bread, broken in pieces and distributed among His disciples, represented His body. The wine represented "my blood of the covenant, which is poured out for many" (Mk. 14: 22–24). There is no doubt that with the word of Jesus spoken over the wine we are taken into the realm of sacrifice and death. To speak of blood being poured out is to speak of death, and in particular of sacrificial death. Just as the old covenant made between God and Israel in the wilderness was sealed by a sacrifice, so Jesus announced the inauguration of the new covenant between God and men sealed with His own

[27]J. Jeremias in *Theologisches Wörterbuch zum Neuen Testament*, VI, pp. 536–545.

blood (Ex. 24: 8; Jer. 31: 31–34). At the same time, the use of the words 'for many' shows that Js. 53, where the Servant makes himself an offering for sin and bears the sin of many, is also in mind. The sacrificial language in the word over the bread is less obvious, but the parallelism between the two sayings and the form of the saying recorded by Paul (1 Cor. 11: 24) make it plain that the thought of Jesus' approaching death is present in this saying also.

These two sayings of Jesus Himself bring out most clearly the meaning of His death, as He saw it. They do not stand entirely alone, for alongside them we may place the saying of John the Baptist, "Behold, the Lamb of God, who takes away the sin of the world" (Jn. 1: 29) and the words of Jesus about the good shepherd who "lays down his life for the sheep" (Jn. 10: 11). These sayings, along with others (e.g. Jn. 3: 14; 12: 24 f.), show that Jesus saw His death as something far more than an act of courageous and final witness to the truth of His message. He regarded it as an act of service for mankind, the offering of a sacrifice and the payment of a ransom through which they might be delivered from sin and death.

This is shown, finally, by the words of Jesus as He died on the cross. When He cried, "My God, my God, why hast thou forsaken me?" (Mk. 15: 34), He expressed His sense of abandonment by God. The later New Testament writers believed that Jesus was 'made to be sin' and that He was under the curse of God as He hung on the cross (2 Cor. 5: 19; Gal. 3: 13). Their teaching provides the explanation of the cry; on the cross Jesus was dying as a ransom for sinners and there endured that exclusion from God which is the consequence of sin.[28]

Seen in this way the cross is more than a tragic accident which was turned to good account. It was not an incongruous conclusion to a life spent in doing good, nor was it merely the last stage in a process of continual opposition to Jesus. It was an integral part of the work which He came to do. Jesus came to the world in order to die, and He freely submitted to the hands of men, knowing that God's purpose was being fulfilled and confident that God would vindicate Him. As He had spoken of His resurrection from the dead, so on the third day He appeared alive to His friends and left them in no doubt that apparent tragedy was divine victory. From then onwards what had lain outside their vision, or at best on the fringe, during the earthly life of Jesus, became the centre of their thought about Him.

[28]See L. Morris, *The Cross in the New Testament* (1965), pp. 42–49.

We ourselves, looking back from the same vantage-point after Easter, can understand that the death and resurrection of Jesus formed the decisive stage in the coming of the kingdom which had been the main theme of Jesus' message. It was the supreme act in which God intervened to overthrow the forces of sin and death and brought salvation to mankind. To say this is not to deny that God had acted in kingly power before the cross so that men and women genuinely experienced the blessings of His salvation. It was, however, only through the gateway of death and resurrection that the kingdom could come with power, and it is interesting that the link between the kingdom and the cross is made in the enigmatic saying of Jesus at the last supper: "Truly, I say to you, I shall not drink again of the fruit of the vine until that day when I drink it new in the kingdom of God" (Mk. 14: 25). The death of Jesus, as His self-giving for the many, and the resurrection, as God's vindication of His Servant, thus form together the supreme act in the coming of the kingdom and the culmination of the work of Jesus. From now on the prophecies of Jesus began to be fulfilled, according to which He was exalted to the right hand of God and would come again as the Son of man in power and glory to be the judge of men. The development of these thoughts, however, carries us forward beyond the teaching of Jesus Himself to the new estimate of His work to which the Spirit guided His followers in the early Church.

Three

The Risen Lord

T WO GREAT FACTS DOMINATED THE MINDS OF THE FIRST CHRISTIANS
There can be no doubt that the thing about Jesus which most
impressed His followers in the earliest days of the Church was His
resurrection. The life of a man who spoke in God's name and showed
high moral character was not entirely unprecedented during the era
of the early church. We know, for example, how highly the Qumran
sect esteemed their Teacher of Righteousness. Nor was crucifixion
by any means an unusual event in those cruel times. But for a man
to rise from the dead was totally unprecedented. Dead men do not
come to life again. Most pious Jews, with the signal exception of the
Sadducees, hoped that there would be a general resurrection of the
dead at the end of the age, and one might especially hope that a just
man who had suffered innocently would be rewarded by God, but
such hopes remained nothing more than hopes. The fact that Jesus
was *known* to be alive 'by many infallible proofs' (Acts 1: 3) sud-
denly transformed hope into certainty. He had been seen to die by
reliable witnesses; He had equally clearly been seen to be alive.[1] The
general resurrection of the dead had been surprisingly anticipated.
It is not too much to say that the resurrection of Jesus was an event
which filled the minds of the disciples from the first moment when
it was reported. Later, a more balanced perspective would replace
what could have become a one-sided emphasis on this event, but at
the beginning the stupendous nature of what had happened completely overwhelmed the disciples. Imagine, for example, what
would happen if some well-known personality of our own day were
to be seen alive a couple of days after his funeral!

To be sure, the resurrection was not seen primarily as the work of
Jesus. The language of the first Christians shows that they were
conscious that it was God the Father Himself who exercised His

[1]See J. N. D. Anderson, *The Evidence for the Resurrection* (1950); E. M. B.
Green, *Man Alive* (1967).

mighty power in raising His Son from the dead 'because it was not possible for him to be held by it' (Acts 2: 24). As an act of God, however, the resurrection demonstrated the true nature of the work of Jesus. Early Church theology was resurrection theology.

The other fact which dominated the early Church was the coming of the Holy Spirit. To disciples who had scarcely recovered from the shock of Easter the Day of Pentecost brought a transcendent experience of divine power which convinced them that Jesus was still at work: "He has poured out this which you see and hear" (Acts 2: 32). The disciples found themselves filled with a spiritual dynamic. So many people were added to their number by the witness which they gave that in a short time the Church had become a sizable institution. The age of the Spirit had dawned, and, even if Jesus was no longer physically present, the working of the Spirit was permanent proof that His activity had not ceased. Rightly does Luke record at the beginning of Acts that in his Gospel he had related "all that Jesus *began* to do and teach". The early Christians were sure that in their own preaching the risen Christ was confronting men.[2] Signs and wonders too, similar in character to those wrought by Jesus, continued to be performed in His name; the lame were cured, the sick were healed, demons were cast out, paralytics were restored, and the dead were raised (Acts 3: 1–10; 4: 15 f.; 9: 32–43). If the theology of the early Church was resurrection theology, it was equally Holy Spirit theology, for it was through the Spirit that the risen Jesus continued His work.

The Early Preaching

How can we find out the way in which the earliest Christians saw the work of Jesus? We have two sources of information. Our older source is the New Testament Epistles, written by a number of authors from about AD 50 onwards. Jesus was crucified in AD 30 or thereabouts, so that a period of some twenty years separates the beginning of the Church from its earliest surviving literary records. But it is possible by careful scrutiny of the Epistles, especially those of Paul, to detect where the writers are incorporating earlier material

---

[2] This is not to imply that they made no distinction between His words spoken on earth and the Spirit-inspired utterances of Christian prophets. The use of this assumption to justify the radical thesis that the Gospels contain both types of utterance indiscriminately attributed to Jesus is ill-founded.

in their letters. The writings of Paul are not the product of his own creative genius working, as it were, in a vacuum, with no contact with the Christians who preceded him. Paul did not invent Christian theology; although he made many profound advances in Christian thought, he learned the essentials of the faith from other Christians who were, as he said, "in Christ before me" (Rom. 16: 7). He met the disciples in Damascus and Antioch; he visited Jerusalem. Often it is possible to tell where he is using phraseology that he has inherited and to reconstruct in some measure the theology of the early Church which he has preserved. Some of this material has attained the rounded forms of creed and liturgy, and some of it betrays signs of development in an Aramaic-speaking or bi-lingual environment; such facts indicate that we are being given glimpses of precious, early formulations of Christian belief.[8] Alongside Paul we should also mention Peter. His First Epistle, though written later than some of Paul's Epistles, contains such marks of early Christianity and it includes so much material on our theme that we are justified in giving it fairly full and separate consideration in the next chapter.

On the other hand, we have in the Acts of the Apostles a number of summaries of sermons and other discourses by early Christians. Some scholars have argued that these sermons give us not the actual words of the early preachers but what the author of Acts writing at a later date *imagined* that they must have said; they hold that the sermons give us more information about the theology of a later generation than of the early Church.[4] So sceptical a verdict is unwarranted. While it is true that Luke has written up the sermon in his own distinctive style and made a careful choice in his material so that the various discourses are complementary to one another and present a pattern for his readers to imitate, the fact remains that the general content of the sermon accords well with what we can learn about the preaching of the early church from our other sources. There is no reason to suppose that Luke did not inquire as closely as possible of his friends to discover what was actually said. We may very well believe that he was no less careful than the greatest of Greek historians, who wrote: "As for the speeches made by various persons either on the eve of the war or during its actual course, it was difficult for me to remember exactly the words which I myself heard, as also for those who reported other speeches to me.

[8] A. M. Hunter, *Paul and His Predecessors* (1961²).
[4] So, for example, M. Dibelius, *Studies in the Acts of the Apostles* (1956).

But I have recorded them in accordance with my opinion of what the various speakers would have had to say in view of the circumstances at the time, keeping as closely as possible to the general gist of what was really said" (Thucydides, 1 : 22).[5]

When we put together the information derived from these sources, we find that we can reconstruct the kind of 'sermon outline' that must have been in the mind of many a preacher in the early Church. There is a common pattern traceable in the sermons of Peter in Acts which agrees closely with the summary of the Gospel which Paul says that he preached (1 Cor. 15: 3–5). This pattern was roughly as follows:

> "You (the Jews) put Jesus to death,
>> But God raised Him from the dead,
>>> and exalted Him as the Christ.
>> The Scriptures foretold that this was to happen,
>> And we are witnesses that it took place in this way.
>> Repent, therefore, and receive the salvation which is offered to you.
>> Remember that Jesus will return as your judge."

Recent manuscript discoveries have shown that C. H. Spurgeon used to preach sermons considerably longer than the usual modern variety ('Preach about God, and preach about twenty minutes!') from notes even briefer than these. It will be apparent, therefore, that the pattern needed much filling out and that there was much scope for individual development of the basic themes. We must now see how the pattern was developed with regard to the work of Jesus.

The Earthly Life of Jesus

We observe first that the preaching of the early Church had as its basic theme the work of Jesus and its consequences for mankind. Moreover, under the influence of the events of Good Friday and Easter the first preachers concentrated their attention on the death and resurrection of Jesus. The central significance of this double event was never lost in the early Church. For a different outlook, which put more stress on the earthly life of Jesus and especially on

[5]For a conservative estimate of the sermons in Acts see R. H. Mounce, *The Essential Nature of New Testament Preaching* (1960).

His preaching ministry, we have to wait for the period of modern liberal Protestantism. This attitude found its most attractive expression in the famous and influential book by T. R. Glover, *The Jesus of History*. Glover's book represented a reaction against the kind of Christianity which so concentrated its attention on the heavenly Son of God as to ignore the earthly Jesus. It was certainly a necessary protest against an over-emphasis, but, as so often happens, it went to the opposite extreme. There can be no doubt whatsoever that in the New Testament the death, resurrection and heavenly work of Jesus were at the centre of Christian proclamation and theology. One has only to note how rare are the references to the earthly life of Jesus in the Epistles in order to see where the accent lies. Nevertheless, the earthly ministry of Jesus was not forgotten, and it was seen to be of a piece with the death and the resurrection. The early Church knew no modern distinction between historical and so-called trans-historical events, such as the teaching of Jesus and His resurrection respectively.

This is expressed most fully in the speech of Peter to Cornelius: "You know the word which (God) sent to Israel, preaching good news of peace by Jesus Christ (he is Lord of all), the word which was proclaimed throughout all Judea, beginning from Galilee after the baptism which John preached: how God anointed Jesus of Nazareth with the Holy Spirit and with power; how he went about doing good and healing all that were oppressed by the devil, for God was with him. And we are witnesses to all that he did both in the country of the Jews and in Jerusalem" (Acts 10: 36–39 a).

The sermon sums up the work of Jesus as the preaching of good news accompanied by various signs which demonstrated that the peace which He proclaimed was a reality in the experience of His hearers. Further, by means of the mighty works and wonders and signs which God did through Him among the Jews he was clearly attested to be the Messiah (Acts 2: 22). He was God's servant, holy and righteous (Acts 3: 13 f., 26), sent to bring His blessing first of all to the Jews.

Here we find that the significance of the earthly ministry is neatly expressed. What we have in effect is a summary of the contents and structure of the later Gospels. Although the need felt by preachers of the gospel to non-believers was not the only factor which led to the writing of the Gospels, we can see how it must have played a central role in this process. It is obvious that a sermon outline, such as that of Peter, would have been filled out with particular incidents and examples of the sayings of Jesus from the stock of traditions that was to hand throughout this period in the Church in Palestine.

The Crucified Messiah

It is probable that in much of the preaching of the early Church, directed as it was to the Jews, the purpose in presenting the earthly life of Jesus was to supply the framework for the account of His death. It was precisely this *good* man whom the Jews had put to death. They rejected the 'Author of life', and asked for a murderer to be released to them, although Pilate had pronounced Jesus to be innocent (Acts 3: 13–15). More than that, they had rejected the One whom God had attested to them by His mighty works (Acts 2: 22).

From this point of view the death of Jesus was not so much a 'work' which He performed as rather the unfortunate fate which the Jews had prepared for Him. Nevertheless, it was firmly held that the death of Jesus was God's way for Him. What took place apparently by the free choice of the Jews was at the same time the fulfilment of the divine plan for Jesus (Acts 2: 23). His death was "according to the Scriptures" (1 Cor. 15. 3). "What God foretold by the mouth of all the prophets, that his Christ should suffer, thus he fulfilled" (Acts 3: 18). Ultimately, Herod and Pontius Pilate simply accomplished "whatever thy hand and thy plan had predestined to take place" (Acts 4: 27 f.; cf. 8: 32–35).

We can readily understand why the early Church stressed this point in its preaching to the Jews. The Christians firmly believed that Jesus was the Messiah. They had, therefore, to explain how a man who had died ignominiously by crucifixion could be the chosen of God. Their answer had two parts. The first part was that the Old Testament, properly understood, prophesied that the Messiah must suffer. It is a moot point whether the Jews at this time believed in the possibility of a suffering Messiah, but on the whole it is unlikely that this was a widely held belief.[6] The early church, therefore, had to show from the Scriptures that suffering was prophesied for the Messiah if it was to overcome this *prima facie* objection to the proclamation that the Messiah was Jesus. The early preachers saw such prophecy in the words of Ps. 2: 1–2 (Acts 4: 25 f.) which spoke of the rulers of the world setting themselves against God and His

[6]H. H. Rowley, *The Servant of the Lord* (1952).

Messiah, and in the prophecy of the suffering Servant which Philip expounded to the Ethiopian chancellor (Acts 8: 32–35). More generally, they were prepared to argue, as Stephen did, from the general tendency of the Jews to reject divine messengers to their betrayal and murder of Jesus (Acts 7: 51–53).

The Risen Lord

The other part of the Church's answer to Jewish objections was of course the resurrection of Jesus. We can divide their argument here into two sections. In the first place it was essential to stress the *factuality* of the resurrection. The 'sermon-outline' of the early preachers assigned an important place to the role of the witnesses to the resurrection. Paul's preaching stressed that "Christ died . . ., that he was buried, that he was raised on the third day in accordance with the scriptures, and that he appeared to Cephas and then to the twelve . . . He appeared also to me" (1 Cor. 15: 3–8). The same note of witness runs through the preaching in Acts: "This Jesus God raised up, and of that we are all witnesses . . . We cannot but speak of what we have seen and heard" (Acts 2: 32).[7]

There can be no doubt that the purpose of this continued repetition of the fact that there were eyewitnesses who had seen the risen Jesus was to give proof that the resurrection was a real historical event. But is the proof a sound one?

We possess good evidence in the New Testament (with some supplementation from other sources) that Jesus died as a result of crucifixion and was buried in or around Jerusalem on a spring day probably in A.D. 30.[8] There is equally good evidence that many people believed that they had seen Him alive for a period from the third day after His death onwards, and also that His tomb was found to be empty. These are the data that must be explained in terms of some historical fact.

Christians affirm that the most reasonable historical explanation of the data is that Jesus did recover life after being dead and was seen alive by His friends. This is to say that the resurrection itself was a historical event, in the sense that it actually happened at a particular time and in a particular place, in exactly the same way as

[7]Cf. Acts 3: 15; 4: 33; 5: 32; 10: 40 f.; 13: 21; 22: 15; 26: 16.
[8]The real doubt that exists regarding the precise date of the crucifixion in no way invalidates the basic fact that it really happened.

any other unobserved event which the historian postulates on the basis of its observable consequences.

But is the Christian explanation of the data the right one? Some scholars, who firmly believe that the resurrection actually took place, would say that the evidence for it is not conclusive. (They would also say that there is certainly no conclusive evidence against it.) Others, however, would argue that the evidence is sufficiently compelling to admit of no other conclusion.

The factor which leads many people to doubt or deny the Christian interpretation of the evidence is the presupposition that men do not rise from the dead. This is a natural presupposition, since resurrections are at the best extremely rare occurrences, but it is nevertheless an arbitrary and unsupported presupposition. A historian who works from rationalist presuppositions (such as this one) is bound to deny that the resurrection happened and to seek some other explanation of the evidence. The Christian would insist that his false presuppositions prevent the rationalist historian from giving an adequate evaluation of the evidence, and that, granted that a resurrection is a possibility, the Christian interpretation of the evidence is much more satisfying and coherent.

A historian may protest that a supernatural event, such as the resurrection, which cannot be fitted into the complex of natural causes and effects, must not be allowed in a historical scheme; it is not an ordinary historical event, since history by definition is concerned with the world of natural causes and effects. When, however, as in this case, it makes nonsense of the evidence to explain it in any other way, the so-called 'surd' must be admitted, and the historian must be prepared to allow that there is a different plane of reality in which such an event as the resurrection is not an irrational intrusion.[9]

Such problems as these would not have detained the early Church. They were able to proceed more quickly to the second section of their proof which was a demonstration that in rising from the dead Jesus had fulfilled the Old Testament prophecies regarding the Messiah. The essence of the argument is given in Luke's summary of Paul's preaching in the synagogues: "He argued with them from the scriptures, explaining and proving that it was necessary for the Christ to suffer and to rise from the dead, and saying, 'This Jesus, whom I proclaim to you, is the Christ' " (Acts 17: 2 f; cf. 26: 23).

[9]D. Fuller, *Easter Faith and History* (1968).

The details of this proof occupy large parts of some of the sermons of Peter. We find it expressed in his sermon at Pentecost. There he argued that it was against the nature of things for Jesus to be held captive by death. Why? In Psalm 16: 10 David had said, "Thou wilt not abandon my soul to Hades, nor let thy Holy One see corruption." At first sight these words should have referred to David himself. But there was the obvious objection that David did in fact die and was buried; the words could not be said to have been fulfilled in his case. There must be another explanation, and Peter argued that David was speaking prophetically of one of his descendants whom God had promised to set on his throne. Similarly, the words of David in Psalm 110: 1, "The Lord said to my Lord, 'Sit at my right hand, till I make thy enemies a stool for thy feet' " were not true of the Psalmist himself, but were fulfilled in the exaltation of Jesus to heaven (Acts 2: 24–36).

The same proof is found in the sermon of Paul at Pisidian Antioch (Acts 13: 30–37). Here, however, a reference is added to Psalm 2: 7, where the words "Thou art my Son, today I have begotten thee", were understood to be a reference to the 'begetting' of Jesus to new life by God. The early Church thus found the most appropriate fulfilment of such Old Testament prophecies in the resurrection of Jesus. These scriptural proofs indicated that the resurrection was not simply the resuscitation of a dead man, but the exaltation of Jesus by God as Messiah and Lord.[10]

The New Status of the Risen Jesus

A detailed examination of the status and significance assigned to Jesus as the result of His resurrection belongs more to a study of His person, but something must be said about this here, since the person and work of Jesus are closely bound up together.

For the early church the resurrection was not merely a sign of victory over death (Acts 2: 24, 31 f.). It was the act by which God exalted Jesus to His right hand (Acts 2: 33). Consequently, the resurrection and ascension of Jesus were regarded as one event. Popular Christian thought often regards the resurrection as taking place on Easter Sunday and being followed after forty days by the ascension and exaltation of Jesus. At first sight the New Testament

[10]On the use of the Old Testament in Acts 13 see E. Lövestam, *Son and Saviour* (1961).

seems to support this view, but closer study shows that the early Christians did not regard the ascension as an event separate from the resurrection and subsequent to it. What we call the ascension, as related in Acts 1: 1–11, is, properly speaking, the final appearance of Jesus to His disciples (with the exception of the special appearance to Paul (1 Cor. 15: 8)); the end of the forty-day period was marked by a symbolical ascent. Easter Sunday was the day of resurrection *and* exaltation; our failure to realize this is perhaps because our inability to think in any other than spatial terms makes it hard for us to believe that appearance on earth and exaltation to heaven are compatible modes of existence. An understanding of this point helps to explain why in some parts of the New Testament (e.g. Phil. 2: 6–11; Hebrews) the resurrection is not mentioned and the emphasis falls on the exaltation of Jesus. Resurrection and exaltation are names for one and the same event viewed from two different angles.

The exaltation of Jesus indicated to His followers that He was indeed the Messiah or Christ (Acts 2: 36). The status which Jesus had implicitly claimed for Himself while on earth thus received divine confirmation. This is demonstrated further by the way in which Stephen had a vision of the *Son of man* standing at the right hand of God (Acts 7: 56); Jesus' words about the vindication and resurrection of the Son of man were shown to be true. He was indeed "proclaimed Son of God in all his power through his resurrection from the dead" (Rom. 1: 4 Jer. B; cf. Acts 13: 33; 1 Thes. 1: 10).

If the resurrection confirmed the status which Jesus had claimed for Himself in His earthly ministry and led the disciples into a fuller realization of its significance, it also indicated a new stage in the dealings of God with the Messiah. This is seen in the attribution of the title of 'Lord' (Gk. *Kurios*) to Jesus (Acts 2: 36). With the usage in Ps. 110 for a background it was the obvious title to apply to the exalted Jesus. He was now the 'Lord of all' (Acts 10: 36), and the title became extremely common on the lips of His followers. Most significant in this connection is the early Christian 'hymn' found in Phil. 2: 6–11 which expresses the early church's understanding of the person and work of Jesus.[11] This goes far beyond anything that we have so far examined in the way in which it speaks of the divine

[11]An extremely detailed study of this 'hymn' is given by R. P. Martin, *Carmen Christi* (1967).

nature and status possessed by Jesus before His incarnation in His pre-existent state; then, having described His self-abasement in accepting the status of a slave and showing obedience to the point of death, it proclaims how God 'more than exalted' Him and gave Him 'the name which is above every name' so that all creation might worship and glorify Him. The exalted name is undoubtedly that of 'Lord', and it is significant that the words used to describe the respect paid to Jesus are drawn from an Old Testament passage describing the worship of God (Is. 45: 23). How far the early Church realized the full implications of the title of Lord, which was the name of God in the Greek versions of the Old Testament, at this early date is uncertain; what is certain is that as these implications were more and more recognized they were fully accepted by all except some fringe members of the Church. Jesus was in the fullest sense the Son of God and the heavenly Lord.

The Gift of Salvation

What mattered most to the first Christians was not the metaphysical implications of the titles which we have just discussed but rather the significance of the exalted Jesus for His followers. Personal experience had shown them that in this exalted capacity Jesus was their Saviour. The actual title of 'Saviour' was applied somewhat infrequently to Jesus (Acts 5: 31; 13: 23), and such a synonym as 'the Author of life' (Acts 3: 15; 5: 31) is likewise rare at this period. Nevertheless, the fact that Jesus saved and offered salvation was clearly known and appreciated.[12]

The gift had various aspects. It represented first of all an opportunity for repentance. Repentance is not an act that a man can perform when he chooses. It is possible only when God Himself announces that He is willing to accept men. Such an opportunity was present in the preaching of the early Church. Peter was prepared to emphasize in no uncertain terms the guilt of the Jews in crucifying Jesus, but at the same time He affirmed his belief that they had acted in ignorance and offered them the chance of repentance (Acts 3: 17–19; 5: 31). According to Jewish law, if a man was caught transgressing the law it was customary merely to give him a warning, on the grounds that he might be ignorant of the law's demands and consequently acting unwittingly; if, however, after the

[12]See for example Acts 2: 21, 47; 4: 12; 11: 14; 13: 26, 47; 15: 11; 16: 30 f.

warning the man committed the same offence, there could be no doubt that he now knew what he was doing and was consequently a wilful transgressor, worthy of punishment. In the same way, the early Church offered the Jews a 'warning' and a chance to repent, lest by continuing in the attitude which had led them to crucify Jesus they should become wilful rejectors of Him. The grace of God offered them the opportunity to turn from their former ways.

Related to repentance, like one side of a coin to the other, is faith. It was the condition of receiving salvation (Acts 10: 43; 1 Cor. 15: 2), not in the sense that it was a 'work' which God demanded as a proof of human worthiness, but rather in the sense that God accompanied His offer of salvation to men with an indication of the way in which they could receive it. Faith meant committal to Christ, and it was outwardly expressed in submission to baptism (Acts 2: 38, 41; 8: 16, 38; et al.). The two aspects of acceptance of salvation are summed up in 1 Thes. 1: 9 f. which describes the two-fold activity of "turning from idols . . . to serve a living and true God, and to wait for his Son". The language of this verse applies to Gentiles rather than to Jews, but the same structure of response is apparent.

The blessing offered to those who repented is described as "the forgiveness of sins" (Acts 2: 38; 5: 31; 10: 43). Peter commanded his hearers, "Repent therefore, and turn again, that your sins may be blotted out" (Acts 3: 19). Similarly, Paul said, "Through this man forgiveness of sins is proclaimed to you, and by him everyone that believes is freed from everything from which you could not be freed by the law of Moses" (Acts 13: 38 f.). What is not explained in Acts, however, is how forgiveness is connected with Jesus. He appears to be endued with power to forgive the repentant by virtue of His exalted position as God's representative. But A. M. Hunter has observed that the form of words in Acts 5: 30 and 10: 39, which speak of Jesus 'hanging on a tree', goes back to Dt. 21: 22 f. and implies that Jesus 'bore the curse for others'. Moreover, the early Church preserved the teaching of Jesus Himself about the sin-bearing significance of His death.[18] More important is the explicit statement in the early preaching recorded by Paul that "Christ died for our sins" (1 Cor. 15: 3), and this is confirmed by Rom. 3: 24 f. and 4: 24 f. which are also very probably derived from the early

[18]*Interpreting New Testament Theology*, p. 74.

preaching. These texts make it certain that, as far back as we can trace, the early Church saw atoning value in the death of Jesus.

The other main aspect of the gift of salvation was the outpouring of the Spirit. Here the point that interests us is that this gift was regarded as coming from Jesus Himself. Although the prophecy in Joel 2: 28–32 which stood at the beginning of Peter's sermon on the day of Pentecost spoke of *God* pouring out His Spirit upon all flesh and of men calling upon the name of the *Lord* to be saved, Peter stated that it was Jesus who had poured out the promised Spirit, having received this gift from the Father (Acts 2: 33). Rightly does Luke later speak of 'the Spirit of Jesus' (Acts 16: 7).[14] Thus the promise of Jesus to send 'another Counsellor' was fulfilled (Jn. 14: 16).

In this way Jesus was regarded as being still active in the life of the Church. It was by His power that mighty works were performed (Acts 3: 16; 4: 10, 30; 9: 34). He Himself acted to receive His martyr, Stephen, to His presence (Acts 7: 55 f.; Jesus was seen *standing* in welcome) and to reveal Himself to Saul on the road to Damascus (Acts 9: 5–6). This point is not unimportant. It means that from the earliest days the Church was conscious of the continuing work of Jesus in saving His people and caring for them.

The Coming Judge

One further point concludes our discussion of the work of Jesus as it was understood in the preaching of the early Church. In accordance with His promises, the early Church awaited His return from heaven: "This Jesus, who was taken up from you into heaven, will come in the same way as you saw him go into heaven" (Acts 1: 11). His return was associated with both blessing and judgement.

On the one hand, we have the hope expressed by Peter "that times of refreshing may come from the presence of the Lord, and that he may send the Christ appointed for you, Jesus, whom heaven must receive until the time for establishing all that God spoke by the mouth of his holy prophets from of old" (Acts 3: 19–21). With these words Peter looks forward to the messianic era and its blessings. It is the same hope as is expressed in the words of Paul: "to wait for his Son from heaven, whom he raised from the dead, Jesus who delivers us from the wrath to come" (1 Thes. 1: 10).

[14]Cf. Rom. 8: 9; Phil. 1: 19; 1 Pet. 1: 11.

On the other hand, the returning Jesus was "the one ordained by God to be judge of the living and the dead" (Acts 10: 42). The proof of this 'ordination' lay in the resurrection understood as the exaltation of Jesus to be the Lord (cf. Acts 17: 31).

The second coming of Jesus is not mentioned very often in the early preaching, and the lack of emphasis is significant. It does not mean that the second coming was a matter of indifference to the Church, but rather that the historical facts of the resurrection and the outpouring of the Spirit were at the centre of their experience and their message. They were not a fanatical apocalyptic sect, preaching that the end of the world was just round the corner and dangling their hearers over the pit. Although the word 'grace' is rare in documents from this period (the earliest reference in Acts is at 11: 13), the early Church was conscious of the reality expressed by the word and lived in an atmosphere of rejoicing at what Jesus had done for it (Acts 2: 46 f.; 8: 39; 10: 46).

Four

An Example and a Saviour

IN OUR STUDY SO FAR WE HAVE EXAMINED THE TEACHING OF JESUS regarding His own work and the way in which the earliest Christians saw in Him the risen Lord. This gives us a two-fold foundation in the tradition of the ministry of Jesus and the gospel preached by the apostles for our further exposition. From this point onwards Christianity spread in various directions, and a number of different courses might be followed as we attempt to chart the fuller developments of Christian thought about the work of Christ. We propose to devote separate chapters to the writings associated with Paul, the writer to the Hebrews and John respectively, and in the present chapter we shall look at the minor writings of the New Testament – minor, that is, in terms of length. These writings are of uncertain date, and therefore it is worth emphasizing that they are not to be thought of as predecessors of Paul and the other great writers but rather as documents which illustrate parallel developments of thought.

Christ the Teacher

At first sight the Epistle of James has nothing to offer on our subject. It is distinguished from other New Testament documents by its almost total lack of reference to Jesus by name (Jas. 1: 1; 2: 1). It is tempting to argue that its author was no theologian, and some have even gone further and asked whether this is not a Jewish rather than a Christian book.

These criticisms evaporate away once the distinctive aim of the Epistle is recognized. It is not a textbook of theology but a compendium of ethical teaching for Christians. Christian doctrine is here subordinated to practical exhortation, not because it is unimportant but because it is presupposed that the readers are already familiar with it. The teaching of James is for those who have already heard and accepted the gospel message.

In fact there is more Christian theology in James than is some-times thought.[1] The author pins the hopes of his readers upon the future coming of the Lord, i.e. Jesus, who will vindicate the oppressed and judge the sinful (Jas. 5: 7–9). James is also aware of the present power of the Lord to heal the sick and to forgive sins when prayer is made 'in the name of the Lord' (Jas. 5: 14 f.); here again, in a Christian Epistle, 'Lord' is most probably a title for Jesus. In both of these points James' idea of the work of Christ fits in with what we know of the Church's faith from Acts.

Where James breaks new ground in comparison with what we have already discussed is in his ethical teaching. When the various precepts which he offers are carefully examined, it becomes apparent that, although Jesus is rarely mentioned by name, the Epistle is heavily dependent upon His teaching. When James tells his hearers to be doers of the word and not merely hearers, we surely have an echo of the closing words of the Sermon on the Mount (Jas. 1: 22 and Mt. 7: 24 ff.).[2] For James the lasting work of Jesus was that He instructed His followers in true godliness.

Ethical and moral instruction is not to be regarded as an inferior aspect of the work of Jesus in comparison with His deeds for man-kind. It is most intimately linked with His work in reconciling men to God, for it indicates the kind of life with which He is pleased; the teaching of Jesus characterizes the style of conduct which is associated with the Kingdom of God whose coming He announced. For James, the Christian must express in his daily conduct the kind of life which God has communicated to him in his new birth (Jas. 1: 18, 21). For this reason the Epistle of James is a valuable witness to an aspect of the work of Jesus which we might otherwise ignore.

The Sufferings of Jesus

The first Epistle of Peter is much more concerned with the work of Christ than are the other Catholic Epistles. The particular problem which faced the readers of this letter was the possibility of persecu-tion for their faith. It is difficult to tell from the letter just how severe were the sufferings which they might have to endure as a

[1] Cf. Jas. 1: 17 f., 21; 2: 14 ff.; 4: 5–7.
[2] See also Jas. 3: 18 and Mt. 5: 9; Jas. 4: 3 and Mt. 7: 7; Jas. 4: 10 and Mt. 23: 12; Jas. 4: 13 f. and Lk. 12: 16 ff.; Jas. 5: 12 and Mt. 5: 37.

result of being Christians, and how far persecution was actually taking place at the time. Some of Peter's statements suggest that his readers were simply facing insult and obloquy from their pagan neighbours (1 Pet. 2: 12), whereas others suggest that a much more fearsome, fiery trial was imminent (1 Pet. 4: 12–19). Teaching on how to stand firm amid the fear of such happenings is set in the context of a general exhortation to live an upright Christian life. It has been suggested that the Epistle gives the substance of the kind of sermon that was preached on the occasion of the baptism of new converts; whether or not this is so, it certainly contains a compendium of doctrinal and moral teaching that would be especially appreciated by young Christians.[8]

Throughout the letter there is an undercurrent of reference to the earthly life and teaching of Jesus which illustrates the life that Christians ought to lead. A number of passages are best explained as reminiscences of events in the life of Jesus by Peter. He speaks of himself as "a witness of the sufferings of Christ as well as a partaker in the glory that is to be revealed" (1 Pet. 5: 1). The first part of this verse certainly looks back to the passion of Jesus. The second part may well be a reference to the transfiguration (cf. 2 Pet. 1: 16–18) as an earnest of the glory that is to follow the sufferings of Christ and His people (1 Pet. 5: 4). When Peter speaks of those who have not seen Jesus, yet love Him, there may be an implied contrast with the fact that he himself had seen Jesus (1 Pet. 1: 8; cf. Jn. 20: 29). Of especial importance is the passage in 1 Pet. 2: 21–23 which bears the marks of eye-witness testimony to the sufferings of Jesus. Finally, an allusion to the way in which Christ clothed Himself with a towel to wash His disciples' feet (Jn. 13: 1–18) has been thought to underlie the injunction, "Clothe yourselves, all of you, with humility" (1 Pet. 5: 5).

More plentiful are echoes of the teaching of Jesus; a recent study has listed as many as twenty possible allusions to the teaching of Jesus in this Epistle.[4] For Peter the work of Jesus as an example and a teacher was of considerable importance.

This emerges especially in the way in which Peter speaks of the

[8]For all these questions see the survey in D. Guthrie, *New Testament Introduction* (1961–65), III, pp. 95–136.

[4]E.g. 1 Pet. 1: 4 and Lk. 12: 33; 1 Pet. 1: 13 and Lk. 12: 35, 45; 1 Pet. 1: 22 and Jn. 13: 34 f.; 1 Pet. 2: 12 and Mt. 5: 16. See R. H. Gundry, 'Verba Christi in 1 Peter', *New Testament Studies* 13 (1966–67), pp. 336–350.

passion of Jesus as an example for believers to imitate when they are faced with undeserved suffering and persecution. Peter's great theme is that there is no merit of any kind in suffering a punishment that is deserved. "What credit is it, if when you do wrong and are beaten for it you take it patiently?" (1 Pet. 2: 20; cf. 3: 17; 4: 15). It is when a person suffers for doing what is right, and bears his suffering patiently, that he deserves God's approval. As the supreme example of such undeserved suffering he cites the case of Jesus Himself: 'For to this you have been called, because Christ also suffered for you, leaving you an example, that you should follow in his footsteps' (1 Pet. 2: 21). The same argument is found at 1 Pet. 3: 17 f. where an injunction to bear suffering wrongfully inflicted is strengthened by the consideration that "Christ also died for sins once for all, the righteous for the unrighteous", and at 1 Pet. 4: 13 where the readers are told that to suffer 'as a Christian' (1 Pet. 4: 16) is to share in Christ's sufferings.

In both of the passages quoted, however, Peter found it impossible to confine Himself to the thought of the death of Jesus as an example. In the first passage the force of the phrase 'for you' led him on to say, "He himself bore our sins in his body on the tree, that we might die to sin and live to righteousness. By his wounds you have been healed" (1 Pet. 2: 24). Similarly, the second passage tells us that Christ died 'for sins', 'that he might bring us to God'. We are reminded of the similar transition of thought in Mk. 10: 42–45. The thought of Christ's death as an example of innocent suffering is inadequate; it is supremely a means of salvation.

The key-word in Peter's description of the death of Jesus is 'suffer'. About a quarter of all the New Testament occurrences of this word-group are found in this brief Epistle. Frequently it is used of the sufferings of Christians, but it is also found as a kind of technical term for the death of Jesus and the attendant circumstances, in the same way as we speak in English of the 'passion' of Jesus.[5] The accent falls upon the elements of persecution and agony in the fate of Jesus, and His patient bearing of such suffering provides an example for His disciples to follow when they share in His sufferings.

But as we already know from Peter's sermons in Acts, the suffering of Jesus was not simply a fate inflicted by men. The coming of Jesus was predestined before the foundation of the world (1 Pet. 1: 20). Not merely was suffering foretold in the prophets generally (1

[5] 1 Pet. 1: 11; 2: 21, 23; 3: 18 (RV); 4: 1, 13; 5: 1.

Pet. 1: 11), but above all the role of the suffering Servant was fulfilled in Jesus. In no other passage in the New Testament is the
teaching of Is. 53: 12 so fully and clearly applied to the death of
Jesus as it is in the key passage, 1 Pet. 2: 21–25. The situation of
men is that they were like sheep going astray (Is. 53: 6), but now
they have been brought back from the paths of sin. They were
suffering from the scars inflicted by sin, but as a result of the
wounds which were borne by Christ they are healed (Is. 53: 5).
They were the victims of sin and its consequences, but Christ bore
their sins in His body on the tree, and they are delivered from them
(Is. 53: 4, 6, 12).

The thoughts which are derived from Is. 53 at this point are
strengthened by the presence of other Old Testament allusions. We
have already seen how the cross is described as a 'tree' (literally,
'wood') in Acts 5: 30 and 10: 39, and that this term rests ultimately
upon Dt. 21: 22 f. By suffering upon the Cross Christ bore for others
the curse which is due to sin. It is probable also that we should see a
reference to the scapegoat who bore away all the iniquities of the
people of Israel into the wilderness and made atonement for them
(Lev. 16: 21 f.). All these lines of thought converge in presenting the
death of Jesus as a sacrificial act in which He bore the sins of others
on the cross and by dying exhausted their consequences.

It is noteworthy that in this passage Peter does not stop to draw
out the effects of the death of Jesus in terms of forgiveness. Forgiveness is, to be sure, implicit in his statements (especially v. 25), but
his primary point is that the death of Jesus sets men free from sin
in order that they may live righteous lives. As a result of the death
of Jesus they are enabled to say 'good-bye' to sin and live lives
devoted to righteousness. Thus, and only thus, may they in fact
fulfil the example set before them by Jesus.

If this were the only passage in 1 Peter referring to the meaning
of the death of Jesus, it would be sufficient for us to see how Peter
conceived the work of Jesus on the cross. But three times more there
is explicit reference to the death of Jesus, and from a consideration
of these passages we may be confirmed in our conclusion that Peter
saw the death of Jesus as a sacrificial act through which men are
reconciled to God.

In 1 Pet. 3: 18, quoted above, the same thought of Christ dying
for our sins is expressed. Christ is the righteous One (Is. 53: 11) who
dies on behalf of the unrighteous and thus brings them into the

presence of God. Since it is axiomatic in the Bible that the unrighteous cannot come into the presence of God, it follows that the
death of Jesus is the means by which their sin is removed; it is an
offering to God on the basis of which the sinner may be reconciled
to God. Indeed, the words 'for sin' may perhaps be translated 'as a
sin offering'. We note that it is a finished act, performed 'once for
all', a thought which is developed by the writer to the Hebrews.

Another way of expressing the same idea is to employ the
terminology of ransom, with which we are already familiar from
Mk. 10: 45. What Peter brings out more fully than the passage in the
Gospels is that the means of redemption is in fact an act of sacrifice.
The price paid to set Christians free from their futile life of sin was
not silver or gold (cf. Is. 52: 3) but "the precious blood of Christ, like
that of a lamb without blemish or spot" (1 Pet. 1: 19). It is doubtful
whether any one particular type of sacrifice was before the writer's
mind at this point. More probably he saw Jesus as the fulfilment of
the entire Old Testament sacrificial system, but among the particular
passages which he may well have had in mind we should include
the description of the passover lamb (Ex. 12: 5, 13) and the description of the suffering Servant as a lamb led to the slaughter (Is. 53:
7).

It is as a result of such considerations as these that Peter is able
at the very outset of his Epistle to greet his readers as men who
have been chosen by God with a view to "obedience to Jesus Christ"
and "sprinkling with his blood" (1 Pet. 1: 2). This time the imagery
used takes us back to the formulation of the covenant between God
and Israel at Sinai when the blood of a sacrificial animal was
sprinkled upon the people as a token that they gave themselves to
God and intended to be obedient to His commands (Ex. 24: 3–8; cf.
Mk. 14: 24). There may be also an allusion to the similar ritual at
the consecration of priests (Ex. 29: 21; Lev. 8: 30). From a spiritual
point of view, believers may be said to be 'sprinkled' with the blood
of Jesus as a token that they are God's people and are pledged to
obey Him; they are now "a chosen race, a royal priesthood, a holy
nation, God's own people" (1 Pet. 2: 9).

The extent of these references shows what a prominent place the
death of Jesus had in the mind of Peter. We can see how the centre
of gravity in Christian theology had shifted somewhat from the
resurrection to the death of Jesus. Here we have a deep understanding of the death of Jesus which has taken up the clues pre-

served in the Gospel tradition and constructed a doctrine of the righteous and innocent One who suffers a sacrificial death for us in order that we might be reconciled to God, freed from the power of sin, and consecrated to a new life of righteousness.

The Victory of Christ

Although the main emphasis of Peter is upon the death of Christ, the resurrection, which had been so vital in the earliest Christian thought, has by no means lost its importance. At the very outset of the Epistle Peter reminded his readers that they had been "born anew to a living hope through the resurrection of Jesus Christ from the death" (1 Pet. 1: 3). Writing to a world of pagans rather than of Jews, Peter was bearing witness to one of the chief aspects of the deliverance wrought by Christ. The Hellenistic world in general did not believe in the resurrection (Acts 17: 32); at best there was some kind of shadowy existence for the soul. The Christian gospel proclaimed that the resurrection of Christ was proof of a life after death and a heavenly inheritance (1 Pet. 1: 4).

The primitive emphasis upon the resurrection as the vindication of Jesus by God was not forgotten. It is implicit in the way in which the resurrection is associated with the glorification of Jesus (1 Pet. 1: 11, 21) and His enthronement at the right hand of God (1 Pet. 3: 21 f.). But another thought of greater importance for erstwhile pagans now comes to expression. The religious thinking of the ancient world knew of many strange and mighty powers which controlled the universe and the fate of men. The references in the New Testament to 'authorities and powers' are a reflection of these common beliefs. Amid a welter of conflicting theories and concepts one thing was clear: the life of mankind was under the sway of evil, demonic, arbitrary forces, and men longed for deliverance. The Christian answer was that Christ was supreme over all such powers, both real and imaginary. He "is at the right hand of God, with angels, authorities and powers subject to him" (1 Pet. 3: 22). Men no longer need fear their power, especially when it was manifested in the form of persecution through their human instruments.

It is in this context that we are probably to understand the difficult passage in which Peter tells us that at the time when Christ was "put to death in the flesh but made alive in the spirit . . . he went and preached to the spirits in prison, who formerly did not

E

obey, when God's patience waited in the days of Noah" (1 Pet. 3: 18–20). Few passages in the New Testament are as mysterious as this one, and any attempt at explanation is bound to be tentative and incomplete. The 'spirits in prison' have been identified in two ways. One view sees in them a race of fallen angels who had been imprisoned by God (cf. 2 Pet. 2: 4). They would then be the 'sons of God' of Gn. 6: 1–4. The other view is that they were the rebellious generation of Noah's contemporaries who perished in the flood. Some scholars would argue that these two groups cannot be rigidly distinguished from each other. The preaching which was addressed to them has been thought to be a proclamation of the gospel. Support has been found for this view in 1 Pet. 4: 6 which says, "This is why the gospel was preached even to the dead, that though judged in the flesh like men, they might live in the spirit like God." It is argued that this verse speaks of a preaching to the dead, so that they might have the opportunity of salvation; the 'dead' in question would no doubt be the men of the Old Testament (especially of Noah's generation) who lived before the coming of Christ. Though widely supported, this interpretation is unlikely. It is much more likely that Peter is here speaking of men of his own generation who heard and accepted the gospel *before* they died; although they appeared to men to have suffered the judgement of death like every-body else, yet in reality they had been received by God and will live spiritually with Him. If this is the correct view of this verse, it is no longer relevant to the question of the preaching to the spirits in prison. We may then take the content of the proclamation to be that Christ is the victorious Lord to whom all must submit. By His death and exaltation He has become the lord even of the spirits in prison. Thus the passage confirms the fact of His victory over the powers of evil in general, as is stated almost immediately afterwards (1 Pet. 3: 22).[6]

Understood in this way, this obscure passage becomes a testi-mony to the universal scope of the work of Jesus. Its effects were felt even in the underworld and among the powers of darkness. He is indeed the Lord of Lords, and His people need no longer fear the forces arrayed against them. Perhaps there is also the thought that as He proclaimed His lordship to the powers, so believers should not be afraid to bear testimony to the pagans (1 Pet. 3: 14 f.).

[6]For the general view of these difficult verses adopted here see especially E. G. Selwyn, *The First Epistle of St Peter* (1946).

With the victory of the resurrection as a proof of the power and glory of Christ, His people can now look forward to His future coming in glory. This event is described as a 'revelation' (1 Pet, 1: 13; 4: 13; 5: 1, 4), for at present believers walk by faith and not by sight (1 Pet. 1: 8). Their experience of salvation is real, and their joy is beyond description, but at present they share in the sufferings of Christ rather than in His glory. Until that day of revelation, however, they are not cut off from the Christ whom they serve. They form part of a spiritual temple, of which He is the cornerstone, and as spiritual priests they make their offerings to God through Him (1 Pet. 2: 4–6). They obey Him as their Lord (1 Pet. 1: 2; 3: 15 f.), and they find that He watches over them as their Shepherd and Guardian (1 Pet. 2: 25). In a very real sense He can even be said to fulfil the functions of the Father Himself towards them, for very often Peter describes the work of Father and Son in the same terms (cf. 1 Pet. 4: 19; 5: 10).

The work of Christ, therefore, is a continuous work. Between His resurrection and His revelation in glory He is united to His people and they are spiritually dependent upon Him. They are in fact 'in Christ' (1 Pet. 5: 14), a phrase whose full content we have yet to discover when we turn to the Epistles of Paul.

All this shows that the conception of the work of Christ held by Peter is full and rich. The concept of the suffering Servant, which seems at first sight to sum up Peter's view of Christ, is ultimately inadequate for One who was predestined to be Saviour before the foundation of the world, whose mighty work shakes even the realm of the dead, whose care for His people is constant and compassionate, and who will admit them to His glory when He is revealed from heaven. He is indeed worthy to be honoured as Lord (1 Pet. 3: 15).

The Basis for Christian Behaviour

Of the two Epistles ascribed to Peter modern scholarship almost unanimously disallows the second to him and ascribes a late date to it. That the evidence is by no means all on one side has been shown to good effect by E. M. B. Green.[7] It must, however, be admitted that in comparison with the first Epistle the second does not have a great deal to say about our theme.

[7] *2 Peter Reconsidered* (1961); *Second Peter and Jude* (1967).

Like the Epistle of Jude, with which it has a considerable amount of teaching in common, it is concerned with the refutation of a heresy in the early Church which manifested itself especially in immoral behaviour. The heretics appear to have believed in a 'spiritual' salvation, as they called it (cf. the sarcastic reference in Jude 19 to them as men 'devoid of the Spirit'), which freed them from worry about so-called 'sins of the body'. From this 'spiritual' point of view, which laid all the emphasis on direct knowledge of God, they ignored the reality of the historical foundations of Christianity and they were sceptical of the possibility of future judgement.

The reply of Peter to this position was an exposition of those aspects of the work of Christ which stood in direct antithesis to these heretical assumptions. He has in this respect a more developed and positive point of view than Jude who is mainly (but by no means exclusively) concerned to attest the reality of the judgement of God by reference to past examples and specific prophecies. Both writers address themselves primarily to the faithful Christians, urging them not to fall away but rather to continue patiently in "the faith which was once for all delivered to the saints" (Jude 3). Peter's positive exposition follows four lines of approach.

First, he insisted that the Christian faith is based on historical events and not upon myths and fables such as were found in the pagan, gnostic religions beloved of the heretics. The fact that Jesus had received divine attestation as the Son of God on the mount of transfiguration was vouched for by the presence of the disciples as eye-witnesses. This historical event should be a guarantee that Jesus would return in power and glory (2 Pet. 1: 16–21).

Second, Peter argued that immoral behaviour by so-called Christians is a denial of "the Master who bought them" (2 Pet. 2: 1; cf. Jude 4). In this phrase is summed up that doctrine of the work of Jesus which we found in His own teaching (Mk. 10: 45) and which recurs in 1 Pet. 1: 18; 1 Cor. 6: 20; 7: 23 and Rev. 5: 9. The death of Jesus upon the cross is seen as the payment of a ransom-price to set men free from the tyranny of sin. But those who are set free are at the same time set under the lordship of the One who redeemed them, and they owe obedience to Him. Jesus is both their Saviour and their Lord (2 Pet. 1: 1 f., 11; 2: 20; 3: 2, 18; cf. Jude 4). The juxtaposition of these two titles shows that they go hand in hand and cannot be separated from each other. The person who would enjoy the salvation offered by Christ must acknowledge Him as his Lord.

Those who have been saved are reminded, thirdly, that they escaped from the defilements of the world through "the knowledge of our Lord and Saviour Jesus Christ" (2 Pet. 2: 20; cf. 1: 2, 8; 3: 18). The Christian is to grow in this knowledge (2 Pet. 3: 18). In this phrase it is made clear that for Peter the essence of Christianity is a personal relationship to a living Saviour; what is here called 'knowledge' is very near to what is elsewhere called 'faith'. Such a relationship to the One who called them (2 Pet. 1: 3) commits Christians to a life that grows in godliness and grace (2 Pet. 1: 3–9). To have a personal relationship to Christ is incompatible with continuance in sin. The heretics' denial that Christian faith affects behaviour is thus seen to be false.

Finally, Peter bids his readers to set their hope on the future coming of Jesus. They are to look forward to the eternal kingdom which He will set up at His coming; they must prepare themselves for a realm which will be characterized by righteousness (2 Pet. 1: 11; 3: 11–13; Jude 20). To the scoffers' objection that much time has elapsed with no indication that the kingdom is coming, Peter replies that the apparent delay is a sign of the mercy of the Lord who is not willing even for heretics to perish (2 Pet. 3: 9).

In this way Peter makes use of the common Christian doctrine of the work of Christ for the practical purpose of enabling his readers to discern the true nature of heresy and equip themselves against it. The great facts of the work of Christ – His death on the cross, His present Lordship of His people, and His future coming in mercy and judgement – are seen to be relevant to daily behaviour and all play a part in the task of leading the people saved by Christ "to his own glory and excellence" (2 Pet. 1: 3).

Five

Christ for Us: Christ in Us

T HE TEACHING OF PAUL ABOUT THE WORK OF CHRIST WAS NOT fundamentally different from that of the early church.[1] We have already seen how the information which we obtain from Acts about the preaching of the first Christians is supplemented by various remarks in the Epistles of Paul in which he makes it clear that he fully accepted the teaching which he had received from his predecessors. Although he insisted that his gospel did not come to him through any human channel but through "a revelation of Jesus Christ" (Gal. 1: 12), nevertheless what he taught agreed with the preaching and doctrine of the first apostles. When he spoke to the Corinthian Church of what he had received, he declared that this was the very message which he had also delivered to them in his evangelistic preaching as being "of first importance" (1 Cor. 15: 3). It was a message which centred on the work of Christ, His death, burial and resurrection. Earlier in the same letter he affirmed that his message was summed up in the words "Christ crucified" (1 Cor. 1: 23; 2: 2). Paul's theology was centred upon the saving event of the cross and the resurrection.

The Imitation of Christ

It is no doubt as a result of this emphasis that we find comparatively little information in his letters about the earthly life and teaching of Jesus, although the amount is perhaps larger than is sometimes thought. The essential facts about the life of Jesus are alluded to by Paul. He is able to tell us that Jesus was a man (Rom. 5: 15; 1 Cor. 15: 21), born of a woman (Gal. 4: 4), born as a member of the Jewish race under the law (Rom. 9: 5; cf. 1: 3; Gal. 3: 16). He had a number of brothers, including James (1 Cor. 9: 5; Gal. 1: 19). He exercised a

[1]For the relationship of Paul's teaching to that of Jesus see A. M. Hunter, *The Gospel according to St Paul* (1966), ch. 7.

ministry among the Jews (Rom. 15: 8) and had twelve disciples (1 Cor. 15: 5). On the night when He was betrayed, He held a last supper with His disciples, the details of which had been handed down to Paul (1 Cor. 11: 23–25). He suffered at the hands of the Jews (1 Thes. 2: 15) and under Pontius Pilate (1 Tim. 6: 13), and was put to death by crucifixion (1 Cor. 2: 8) at the time of the passover (1 Cor. 5: 7). After burial He rose from the dead and appeared to various reliable witnesses (1 Cor. 15: 3–5). Paul is able to tell us that His character displayed grace (2 Cor. 8: 1; cf. 1 Cor. 13: 4–7; see below), meekness and gentleness (2 Cor. 10: 1), matched by endurance (2 Thes. 3: 5) and obedience to God (Rom. 5: 19; cf. Phil. 2: 7). There are also a considerable number of allusions to the teaching of Jesus scattered through the Epistles.[2]

It has sometimes been asserted, on the basis of 2 Cor. 5: 16, that Paul had no interest in a Jesus 'after the flesh', i.e. the human Jesus; all that he cared about was the risen and exalted Lord. The view rests upon a misunderstanding of the text; what Paul really said was that he was not interested in a purely human estimate of Jesus, such as he had held before his conversion. The evidence just cited shows that Paul was familiar with the basic facts about the life of Jesus. What he realized clearly was that the work of Jesus in Galilee and Judea affected only the people influenced by it at the time; a gospel meant for the wider world must have as its content the work performed by Christ on the cross through which He gained a cosmic significance. In any case, the task of expounding the significance of the life and teaching of Jesus could be left to those who had known Jesus 'in the days of his flesh' and were better qualified to do so.

When Paul does refer to the earthly life of Jesus, he sometimes uses it as an example for his readers to follow. In Rom. 15: 1–3, when he was encouraging his readers to aim at the good of their neighbours instead of simply pleasing themselves, he clinched his argument by asserting, "For Christ did not please himself". It seems likely that the same train of thought is to be discovered in Phil. 2: 1–11. The first part of this passage contains an appeal to the Christians at Philippi to live in unity with each other, and Paul argues that their disunity springs from selfishness and conceit. In the second part of the passage he quotes what is now recognized to be a 'hymn' which describes the humiliation and exaltation of

[2]E.g. 1 Cor. 7: 10; 9: 14; 1 Tim. 5: 18; possibly I Thes. 4: 15–17; cf. Rom. 13: 7–10 with Mk. 12: 13–17, 28–31; see also Acts 20: 35.

Jesus in His incarnation and ascension. Probably the original purpose of the hymn was to celebrate the saving work of Jesus, but in its present context the hymn is obviously used to strengthen the ethical exhortation in the preceding verses. The precise manner in which it is used is uncertain, since the translation of the linking verse 5 is by no means self-evident.[8] Some scholars would hold that humility is the characteristic that ought to be found in men who now acknowledge Christ as Lord in virtue of His exaltation by God. It is, however, hard to resist the impression that here, as in Rom. 15: 3, Christ is at the same time presented as an example for the Philippians to follow. To be sure, the situations of Christ and His followers are entirely different, but it is the same basic attitude which is required in each. It has been objected that on this view of the passage verses 9–11 have no relevance to Paul's appeal or perhaps suggest to the readers that humility will reap its deserved reward. This, however, is unlikely. Although these verses go on beyond the immediate point at issue, Paul quotes them because they form part of the hymn. They teach not that reward is the bribe to induce us to virtue but rather that God honours those who honour Him. A further parallel to this exhortation is to be found in 1 Cor. 10: 31–11: 1, where Paul warns his readers against giving any offence to other people which might hinder them from being saved. "Be imitators of me," he said, "as I am of Christ." There is probably here also the thought of submission to the commands of Christ through the apostle, but at the same time there is certainly the fact of an example to be followed (cf. 1 Thes. 1: 6).[4]

Christian love also finds its supreme illustration in the life of Jesus Himself. Christians are to forgive one another as God forgave them, and to walk in love, as Christ loved them and gave Himself up for them (Eph. 4: 32–5: 2). When they have complaints against their fellow-Christians, they are to forgive them, just as the Lord forgave them (Col. 3: 13). When Paul describes the lineaments of Christian love in 1 Cor. 13: 4–7 it is a likely guess that it was his Master who sat for the portrait.

Finally, Jesus is an example of fortitude. When Paul speaks of Him "who in his testimony before Pontius Pilate made the good

[8]The meaning is probably, 'Think in this manner, which you also see (or which was also the case) in Christ Jesus'; cf. RV rendering.

[4]For the interpretation adopted here see my review of R. P. Martin, *Carmen Christi*, in *Tyndale Bulletin* 19 (1968), pp. 104–127.

confession", the implication is that this is how Christians ought to behave when their faith is on trial (1 Tim. 6: 13).

These passages show that we ought not to under-emphasize the importance of the work of Christ in being an example for us to follow. Evangelical Christians have often fought shy of teaching which urges men to live as Christ did, for they think that this is to approach dangerously near to salvation by good works. This fear should be a false one, for the passages in which imitation of Christ is inculcated are addressed to those who are already believers in Christ and have set their footsteps on the path of discipleship. What is remarkable is the way in which the early Church made *Christ* an example to believers; since it never lost sight of the identity of the earthly Jesus and the Lord of glory, it saw nothing incongruous in urging its members to be like Jesus and in longing that Christ would be, as it were, formed in them. (Gal. 4: 19).

Yet, when this is said, it remains true that teaching about the imitation of Christ is far from being central in Paul's teaching, and that in passages which speak of imitation of the earthly Jesus the thought of obedience to the heavenly Lord is also present. The centre of Paul's understanding of the work of Jesus must be sought elsewhere. We must turn our attention to what Christ has done for us.

Christ For Us

One aspect of the work of Christ which is curiously absent from the writings which we have so far examined is its character as an expression of divine love and grace. The gospel is known to be associated with the grace of God[5] and Peter speaks of the mercy of God which is active in the new birth of believers (1 Pet. 1: 3; cf. 2: 10), but a close link between the grace of God and the sacrifice of Jesus is not explicit. It is this aspect of the work of Jesus which makes a first, striking impression upon us as we consider Paul's unfolding of the deeper meaning of the work of Jesus. The death of Jesus was not a matter of logical necessity, the fulfilment of some arbitrarily arranged plan. In it the love of God the Father was to be seen as the controlling motive. "God shows his love for us in that while we were yet sinners Christ died for us" (Rom. 5: 8); these words bring out the wonder that Paul continually found in the cross

[5]Acts 13: 43; 14: 3; 15: 11; 20: 24; 1 Pet. 1: 10; 5: 10.

(cf. Eph. 1: 6). What is true of the Father is also true of the Son: "Christ loved us and gave Himself up for us" (Eph. 5: 2; cf. 5: 25). There is never any suggestion that the Father and the Son were in any way in opposition to each other in this regard, whether by the Son wresting forgiveness from an unwilling Father or by the Father demanding a sacrifice from an unwilling Son. Divine love was operative in the Father and the Son.

Lest we should be in danger of thinking of this love as an abstract principle, Paul explicitly avers its personal nature. "The Son of God loved *me* and gave himself for *me*" (Gal. 2: 20). He can speak of each and every Christian as "the brother for whom Christ died" (1 Cor. 8: 11). No matter what the character of the individual man, no matter how great his unworthiness, Christ died for him. The word 'grace', which flowed from Paul's lips as often as 'love', expresses the fact that we are unworthy of divine love and that God acts freely and spontaneously in loving us. He freely forgives those who have no claim upon Him. God's grace overflowed, as Paul puts it, in saving the one who felt himself to be the foremost of sinners (1 Tim. 1: 14 f.). The whole act of Christ's coming and death was inspired by grace (2 Cor. 8: 9; cf. 2 Tim. 1: 9 f.). Nor is the sphere of its working in any way limited. In Christ "the grace of God has appeared for the salvation of all men" (Tit. 2: 11).

Such love constitutes a powerful appeal to men to make their response to God. Through the death of Christ God makes His appeal to men to be reconciled to Himself (2 Cor. 5: 14–21). He demonstrates the reality of His love by giving His Son to die for sinners (Rom. 5: 8). The man who sees Jesus dying on the cross is meant to ask himself:

> Faint and weary Thou hast sought me,
> On the cross of suffering bought me;
> Shall such grace in vain be brought me?

These words, however, show that the appeal of the cross does not lie simply in the fact that it is the scene of the death of God (Act 20, 28 RV) – a phrase which does not mean in the Bible what some so-called theologians would have it mean. A demonstration of love must have some point and purpose. To use a familiar illustration: if I am walking on a pier with a friend who jumps into the water and then declares that he has done this to show that he loves me, I shall not be impressed. If, however, I am in the water and in danger of drowning, then his act would take on meaning, since it would have the purpose of rescuing me from death. Unless the work of Jesus is somehow related to my need, then it cannot be a true demonstration of love. A logic-chopper might argue that my friend's apparently purposeless dive into the water could be a demonstration of what he would be prepared to do out of love for me if I were to be in danger of drowning, but this does not really affect the issue. In this case, his act is still related, even if only potentially, to a real situation of human need. The teaching of Paul, however, makes it plain that the work of Christ really was concerned with an existing need of mankind.

The character of this need is familiar. It is caused by human sin. "Christ died for our sins" is a statement already found in the early, apostolic preaching (1 Cor. 15: 3).[6] For Paul sin is a slavemaster holding sway over men (Rom. 6: 12–22), so that they are unable to escape from its clutches. "Sin pays a wage, and the wage is death" (Rom. 6: 23 NEB).[7] The man who yields to sin finds himself to be at enmity with God; he stands under God's judgement and condemnation, and he is exposed to the wrath of God (Rom. 1: 18; 5: 10). It is in this situation that the death of Jesus provides the answer to human need.

One important clue to the meaning of the death of Jesus is supplied in Gal. 3: 10–14 where Paul speaks of Christ having become a curse for us. 'Curse' here means 'the object of a curse' or 'an accursed thing', a startling phrase which owes its origin to statements in Dt. 21: 23 and 27: 26. Two ideas are brought together by Paul. One is that any person who does not fulfil the law of God stands under a divine curse for his disobedience. Such a person was subject to the sanctions of the law. The other idea is that the body of a man who suffered death by hanging was regarded as accursed, and had to be removed as quickly as possible so that the land would not be defiled. As one whose body had been hung on a 'tree', Jesus stood under the divine curse, and Paul drew the conclusion that He bore this curse as a result of sin. It could perhaps be argued that Paul reached this conclusion by arbitrarily bringing together two proof-texts because of the common word 'curse'. In reality something deeper led to Paul's conclusion. Behind his use of Scripture lay the conviction that Christ, who was Himself innocent, had taken

[6]Cf. Rom. 8: 3; Gal. 1: 4; cf. 1 Pet. 3: 18.
[7]Cf. Rom. 7: 5, 11, 13, 24; 8: 2.

upon Himself the sins of men and undergone all that was associated
with sin, so that men might be set free from their sin and all its
consequences. His starting-point was that Christ came 'in the likeness of sinful flesh'; He who knew no sin was made to be sin for our
sakes (Rom. 8: 3; 2 Cor. 5: 21). The scriptural idea of the curse
brought out vividly the way in which Christ thus took the place
of sinners and endured the consequences of their sin so that they
were redeemed from sin. This basic idea was developed in a number
of ways.

Justification and Forgiveness

In the course of his discussion of the curse of the law Paul uses a
word which has often been seen as one of the key concepts in his
theology. 'Justification' is a word which is connected with the idea
of law.[8] Paul raises the question of whether a man can be justified
before God by the law. That is to say, can a sinner be regarded as
righteous by God on the basis of deeds done in obedience to God's
commands expressed in the law? The word 'justify' thus refers to
the expression of a legal verdict; properly it means to 'acquit', and
it is not concerned with whether the person concerned has a
righteous character. It is concerned with a relationship to God. Is
a man who has sinned in the past acquitted by God if he has kept
the commands of the law? Paul's answer to this question is 'No'.
Complete obedience to the law was required, and no man could
show this. All alike were, and are, sinners (Gal. 3: 22). No human
being will be justified in God's sight by keeping the law (Rom. 3:
20).

How then can a person be justified? If his sin cannot be wiped
out by keeping the law, what other way is there? For an answer
Paul again turns to the Old Testament. In the law itself there was
provision for the sinner to offer sacrifice to God for his sin so
that the sin might be cancelled and the sinner might be forgiven by God. There was a sacrificial system of considerable
complexity which covered various different types of sin and
sinner. Using this language, Paul asserted that the death of Jesus
was a sacrifice for sin. He described it as an 'expiation' or (with

[8]Word studies of 'justification' and other key words in the doctrine of the
work of Christ are given by L. Morris, *The Apostolic Preaching of the Cross*
(1955).

the older translations; e.g. RV) 'propitation' to be received by faith
(Rom. 3: 25).

Considerable controversy has raged over the meaning of this
word. 'To propitiate' means to appease an offended person so that
he is willing to forgive. As used in pagan religious language, the
word described attempts to placate angry gods who broke out in
judgement against men. To speak in such terms of the sacrifice of
Christ might suggest that God is as capricious as a pagan deity.
Consequently, a number of writers have argued that the translation 'to propitiate' is false. They have pointed to the fact that the
use of the word-group in the Old Testament suggests the alternative
translation 'to expiate'. 'Expiate' is a verb which has as its object
not a person but a thing; the purpose of a sacrifice is to expiate sin,
i.e. to wipe it out, or to cancel it, so that it no longer stands between
the sinner and God. More recent research, however, has raised
doubts about the adequacy of this new translation. It has been
observed that very often (as here in Rom. 1: 18–3: 20) the wrath of
God is mentioned in the context of the word. Sin needs to be dealt
with just because it arouses the wrath of God. Furthermore, to
speak of expiating sin is to use a sub-personal category of interpretation. It is to make 'sin' into a thing which can be removed or
effaced. Religion, however, is not concerned with 'things' but with
personal relationships between men and their Creator. It is the
situation of alienation between men and God which must be overcome, and it can be overcome only through some act which re-
stores fellowship between God and sinners; it is not some 'thing'
but the barrier of enmity and guilt which must be removed. Only
the translation 'propitiate' does justice to the personal effects of sin.
One suspects that the attraction of the alternative translation lies in
the way in which it allows the wrath of God against sinners to be
quietly forgotten or even loudly denied. The word 'propitiate' does
affirm the reality of the wrath of God as His holy reaction to sin,
but the paradoxical feature is that according to Paul it is God Himself who puts Jesus forward as a propitiation for sin. Mercy and
judgement meet in the death of Jesus. The holy God who reacts
against sin shows His mercy towards sinners by giving His own Son
as a sacrifice for sin.[9]

Thus it is that Paul can declare that God is both just and the One

[9]See L. Morris, *op cit.* Cf. D. Hill, *Greek Words and Hebrew Meanings* (1967),
ch. 2.

who justifies or acquits sinners (Rom. 3: 26). Since a sacrifice has been offered, the barrier of sin no longer stands, and the sinner may be forgiven. The sacrifice is an act of divine grace. Men do not, indeed they cannot, make an offering to God for their sins. God Himself provides the perfect sacrifice, for He who gives His Son up to death (like Abraham, Gen. 22: 12; Rom. 8: 32) gives us everything in Him.

Justification is thus an act of forgiveness based on what Christ has done for the sinner. It represents a divine verdict upon the sinner rather than a change in the sinner himself. And yet there is a change in the sinner. For it is not every sinner who is justified, even though the benefits of the sacrifice of Jesus are available for all sinners. It is the man 'who has faith in Jesus' who is justified. Just as under the Old Testament law the sinner had to bring his sacrifice and confess his sin over it, so too the sinner must make the sacrifice of Christ his own. There must be faith in Christ, just as Abraham put his faith in God (Rom. 4). When a person accepts Christ in this way, he is reckoned by God to be righteous. It is not that having faith is tantamount to being righteous, as a superficial reading of Paul's words might suggest; rather the person who abandons all claims of his own to God's favour and simply accepts what Christ has done for Him is regarded by God as righteous on the basis of His own gracious act in Christ.

The sinner is thus righteous in the sense that so long as he trusts in Christ who died for Him God will not impute his sin to him. It is as though the last judgement had been anticipated, and the final verdict has already been spoken in his favour. The sinner has, as it were, died with Christ, and the law of God can hold no condemnation against a man who is dead. He has been raised from the dead with Christ, so that he now has the possibility of a new life of righteousness in which the law is fulfilled by the power of the Spirit (Rom. 8: 1–4). Christ has become his righteousness, i.e. the One through whom he is acquitted and forgiven by God (1 Cor. 1: 30).

The significant point for us in all this is the fact that the means of justification is the death of Christ considered as a sacrifice for sin. This is perhaps the most common way in which the New Testament as a whole understands the death of Jesus. When it is remembered that crucifixion was a comparatively bloodless manner of death (the victim died through exposure and exhaustion rather

than through loss of blood by wounds), it is remarkable that time
and again the New Testament writers speak of 'the blood of Christ'.
The source of this imagery undoubtedly lies in the interpretation of
the death of Christ as a sacrifice, and goes back to the words of
Jesus Himself at the last supper. All the imagery of Old Testament
sacrifice is used to bring out the meaning of the death of Christ.
Paul speaks of Him as the passover lamb (1 Cor. 5: 7), and many
scholars have detected an allusion to the Old Testament sin offering
(Lev. 4: 3) in Rom. 8: 3 and 2 Cor. 5: 21 (cf. 1 Pet. 3: 18).

The modern reader is perhaps apt to miss the meaning of this
metaphor. The word 'sacrifice' has undergone a subtle semantic
change over the centuries. Today to speak of sacrifice means to give
up something costly for the sake of some person or to further some
aim. A man may sacrifice his life in time of war so that his fellow-
countrymen may be delivered from tyranny, or a student may
sacrifice hours that could have been employed in the joys of sport
in order to gain a better degree. The idea of cost and self-deprivation
is present, but the essential biblical ideas have disappeared. In the
Bible a sacrifice is an *offering* to God. Such an offering was often,
but not always, an *atonement* for sin. These are the ideas which
are associated with the death of Christ in the New Testament. It
was not simply an act of costly heroism; it was an offering made
to God to atone for the sin of the world.

Redemption and Victory

Another way in which Paul speaks of the effects of the work of
Christ is in terms of redemption, a concept which we have already
seen in Mk. 10: 45; 1 Pet. 1: 18; and 2 Pet. 2: 1. The word has the
meaning of 'deliverance', and the background of thought to the
New Testament usage includes the ideas of the emancipation of a
slave and of deliverance from an enemy. In a rather general sense
the word is applied to the future, final redemption of God's people
from the troubles and temptations of their life on earth (Lk. 21: 28;
Rom. 8: 23; Eph. 1: 14; 4: 30). This final redemption, however, is
overshadowed by the thought that God has already redeemed His
people. The idea of redemption is most closely associated with the
thought of justification (Rom. 3: 24; 1 Cor. 1: 30; Gal. 3: 13; 4: 5)
and forgiveness (Eph. 1: 7; Col. 1: 14). The metaphor implicit in the
word implies that a price has been paid in order that captives may

be set free. Greek readers of Paul's writings would be familiar with the method whereby a slave could pay money into the treasury of a temple until he had deposited sufficient to purchase his freedom; there then took place a ceremony by which the god of the temple 'bought' the slave from his master, and he became a free man. At the same time the word had acquired deeper associations through its use in the Old Testament to describe the Lord's acts of deliverance for His people (e.g. Ex. 6: 6). Paul could, therefore, use the word to describe an act of deliverance wrought by God at great cost. He speaks of believers as men who have been delivered from the curse of the law as a result of the work of Christ. Those who were 'under the law' were vainly trying to please God and win eternal life by keeping the law. They had an entirely mistaken idea of the purpose of the law and of the way to obtain divine forgiveness. The death of Christ set them free from this tyranny. Similarly, justification can be said to have been made possible by the redemptive act of God in Christ. If the death of Jesus is a sacrifice for sin, it is at the same time the great price which God paid in order to set His people free from sin and its consequences.

The idea of redemption is thus closely linked with justification and forgiveness, but it also conveys the ideas of deliverance and freedom. The Christian is no longer under bondage to the law or to any other power and he must hold fast to his freedom (Gal. 5: 1). Yet, just as the Greek slave was set free from earthly masters to be (fictitiously) the slave of the god who 'bought' him, so the believer is set free from lawlessness (Tit. 2: 14) to become the slave of Christ. If his redemption means that he is no longer the slave of men (1 Cor. 7: 23), it also includes the obligation: "You are not your own; you were bought with a price. So glorify God in your body." By His act of purchase Christ has been established as Lord.

It has often been remarked that the New Testament does not ask to whom the price of redemption was paid. To suggest that there was a recipient is to push the metaphor beyond its limits. When the New Testament speaks of believers being liberated from bondage to the devil (Heb. 2: 14 f.), it is not because the devil has received a fee for his captives but because he and his evil associates have been defeated. The cross is regarded as the place of his downfall. It is true that Paul speaks of the defeat of the principalities and powers rather than of the devil himself, but there is no doubt that 'the prince of the power of the air' is numbered with them (Eph. 2: 2; 6: 11–12; cf. Col. 1: 13; 2: 15).

There is a close connection between the defeat of these powers and the release of believers from bondage to the law. Satan is the great 'accuser of the brethren', and the evil powers used the law as a means of holding men in bondage. The law in itself is good and right and established by God (cf. Rom. 7: 12), but it had become a barrier between men and God. Consequently, when Paul speaks of the cross as the place where the principalities and powers are disarmed and defeated, he comments also that the bond which stood against us with its legal demands has been set aside by being nailed to the cross, like the *titulus* placed over the head of the condemned man (Col. 2: 14 f.). The claims of the evil powers over men are wrongful claims. No price need be paid for redemption from them; on the contrary, they must be defeated and forced to give up their unlawful prey.

Reconciliation to God

A further idea is used by Paul to explain the significance of the death of Jesus. He uses the word 'reconciliation' to establish positively the fact of the new relationship which is created by the death of Christ. The situation presupposed is that men are alienated from God by their sin, but God is willing to reconcile them to Himself by no longer counting up their sins against them (2 Cor. 5: 19). It is not that God chooses to disregard their sin as if it were of no consequence. Nor is it that He simply appeals to men who think of Him as their enemy to throw down the barriers which exist on their side and realize that He loves them, true though this is. Rather Paul says that for our sakes God made the sinless Christ to be sin, so that in him we might become righteous (2 Cor. 5: 21). Reconciliation takes place when God is able to regard sinful men as righteous, and this is possible through the work of Christ. Because He bore their sin on the cross, it is no longer reckoned against them. Reconciliation is thus closely linked with justification; it is the expression used for the establishment of a new relationship between God and those whom He acquits of their sin. This is made clear in Rom. 5: 9 f. There Paul places in parallelism the statements that we have been justified by the blood of Christ and reconciled by His death. Those who once were God's enemies need now no longer fear His wrath on the day of judgement, for already their reconciliation to Him is an established fact (Rom. 5: 11). They have peace with God as an assured possession (Rom. 5: 1) through 'the blood of his cross' (Col. 1: 20, 22), and they look forward to God's ultimate aim of bringing them into His presence. Moreover, men out of every race, both Jews and Gentiles, are brought together to the cross, and the implication is that they are there reconciled to each other so as to become one people of God (Eph. 2: 15–16).

The Resurrection of Christ

In Rom. 4: 25 Paul states that Jesus our Lord "was put to death for our trespasses and raised for our justification". The grammarians have had some difficulty in deciding the precise meaning of 'for' in the two parallel clauses of this credal formula.[10] Whatever be the interpretation adopted, the fact that stands out is that for Paul the death and the resurrection of Christ are inextricably linked together as one saving event. Paul cannot think of the cross without at the same time thinking of the resurrection; our assurance of acquittal at God's bar depends on "Christ Jesus who died, yes, who was raised from the dead, who is at the right hand of God, who intercedes for us" (Rom. 8: 34). A man is regarded by God as righteous on the ground of his belief "in him that raised from the dead Jesus our Lord" (Rom. 4: 24).

The passages which have just been quoted show that Paul, like the other early Christians, regarded the resurrection as an act of God rather than of Jesus. Thus he speaks of God's great might manifested "when he raised him from the dead and made him sit at his right hand in the heavenly places" (Eph 1: 19 f.).[11]

What is the significance of this great event? We observe, first, that Paul is not greatly concerned to distinguish between the resurrection and ascension of Jesus. They form for him the one event in which God exalted Jesus. As a result, Jesus Christ is now given the title of 'Lord' and is worthy of universal homage (Phil. 2: 9–11). "To this end Christ died and lived again, that he might be Lord

[10]The difficulty is that 'trespasses' and 'justification' are not parallel terms in content. V. Taylor is probably right in stating that, however the two clauses in the verse be interpreted individually, together they mean that 'Jesus died and rose again because of our trespasses and our justification'; *The Atonement in New Testament Teaching* (1945²), p. 67.

[11]Cf. Rom. 8: 11; Gal. 1: 1; Col. 2: 12; 1 Thes. 1: 10.

both of the dead and of the living" (Rom. 14: 9). Consequently, the mark of a Christian was that he was prepared to make the words 'Jesus is Lord' his public confession of faith (1 Cor. 12: 3). The close connection of the Lordship of Jesus with His resurrection, and of both with the experiences of justification and salvation is brought out in Rom. 10: 9 f.: "If you confess with your lips that Jesus is Lord and believe in your heart that God raised him from the dead, you will be saved. For man believes with his heart and so is justified, and he confesses with his lips and so is saved." Thus through the resurrection Christ is established as the Lord and Head of the Church (Col. 1: 18).

The second fact linked with the resurrection of Christ is that in Him death has been overcome, and an assurance has been given to believers that they too will rise from the dead. "Since we believe that Jesus died and rose again, even so, through Jesus, God will bring with him those who have fallen asleep" (1 Thes. 4: 14).[12] As the first to be raised from the dead, Christ is the 'firstfruits' of the dead; that is to say, His resurrection guarantees the resurrection of those who trust in Him (1 Cor. 15: 20). His appearing has "abolished death and brought life and immortality to light through the gospel" (2 Tim. 1: 10).

Union with Christ

A third consequence of the resurrection must be treated at greater length. In some texts where Paul speaks of the resurrection of believers it is not easy to be sure whether he is thinking of an event in the future or an event that is already a reality. When he tells us that "Christ was raised from the dead by the glory of the Father" so that "we too might walk in newness of life", it seems fairly clear that he is thinking of a present experience. In the very next verse, however, when he says that "if we have been been united with him in a death like this, we shall certainly be united with him in a resurrection like his" (Rom. 6: 4 f.), it seems equally clear that his mind has moved to the final resurrection from the dead. With the conjunction of these thoughts we come to one of the most significant aspects of Paul's thought on the work of Christ, his conception of the present work of Christ in believers.

Like the other early Christians Paul was, of course, conscious of

[12]Cf. 1 Thes. 5: 10; 1 Cor. 6: 14; 2 Cor. 4: 14.

the fact that Christ was not inactive during the period between His exaltation and His advent. It would be false to draw such a conclusion from Heb. 10: 12 f., which is concerned simply to stress the fact that Christ's work of offering a sacrifice for sin took place once and for all at Calvary and is now complete. Rather, from His heavenly seat at the right hand of God Christ intercedes for His people (Rom. 8: 34). His power is demonstrated in the Church when it meets together to exercise discipline upon its unruly members (1 Cor. 5. 4); it is at work in the apostles through whom His message is brought to the world (2 Cor. 12: 9; 13: 3 f.).

More characteristic of Paul's thought, however, is his insight that Jesus Christ is active in the lives of all His people so that they may enjoy newness of life. This is a vast and complex theme, which would take us beyond the limits of our present subject, but we may distinguish four aspects of it which are important for our consideration of the work of Christ.

The first of these is that Paul thinks of believers as sharing in the experiences of Christ, and especially in His death and resurrection. In Rom. 6: 1–11 he describes Christians as having been baptized into the death of Christ; their old self has been crucified with Christ, and they have died with Christ. The same thought recurs in Col. 2: 12; here the death of believers with Christ is presupposed (cf. Col. 3: 3), and Paul goes on to say: "you were buried with him in baptism, in which you were also raised with him through faith in the working of God who raised him from the dead". The precise interpretation of these statements is uncertain. One view is that Paul regards the historical death and resurrection of Jesus as a 'corporate' event which included the spiritual death and resurrection of believers; if Christ died for all men, it could be said that all men died in His death (cf. 2 Cor. 5: 14). Another view is that at baptism there takes place a spiritual repetition of the death and resurrection of Christ in the believer; the believer 'dies and rises to new life' in a manner analogous to that of Christ's death and resurrection (Rom. 6: 5). Probably the second of these views is to be preferred. Paul's thought is that Christians are reckoned to have shared in the death and resurrection of Christ when they join themselves to Him by faith. They are united to a Christ who died and rose again, and these experiences repeat themselves in their lives. It is thus the thought of a present union with Christ which is predominant.

A second way in which this truth is expressed is to say that

Christ is 'in' believers. "If Christ is in you, . . . your spirits are alive" (Rom. 8: 10). The 'old I' has died, and it is now as though Christ himself were living in the believer (Gal. 2: 20). He dwells in the hearts of believers (Eph. 3: 17; 2 Cor. 13: 5), and His presence is the guarantee of everlasting life (Col. 1: 27). This means that Christ is now personally active in the 'hearts' of believers. The word 'heart' is of course to be taken metaphorically; what is meant is that the living Christ is united with the believer so that he enjoys both the fellowship of Christ and the power for new life which He imparts.

To talk in these terms is to enter a realm of spiritual realities in which paradox abounds. This is demonstrated by the other two ways in which this new relationship is phrased. For, thirdly, what Paul says about the presence of Christ in the believer is closely paralleled by his statements about the presence of the Spirit of Christ in him. If in Rom. 8: 10 he says that Christ is in the believer, in the immediate context he speaks of the 'Spirit of God' or the 'Spirit of Christ' in exactly the same way (Rom. 8: 9, 11). This does not mean that the Spirit and Christ are to be identified; the independent 'personality' of the Spirit is clearly attested in the New Testament. The point is rather that the Spirit and Christ are so united with each other in the fellowship of the Trinity that the activities of One may be attributed to the Other. We are dealing with spiritual, meta-human relationships in which our rigid distinctions between individual persons are seen to be inadequate modes of expression.

The same point is made by considering Paul's fourth mode of expression. He refers with extraordinary frequency (about 160 times) to believers being 'in Christ' (or 'in the Lord' and other equivalent expressions). The German scholar, Adolf Deissmann, who was the first to draw attention to the supreme importance of this phrase in the theology of Paul, came to the conclusion that it indicated a kind of spiritual atmosphere 'in' which the Christian lives, just as a fish lives 'in the water'. More recent scholars have been less happy about an interpretation which risks making Christ into an atmosphere rather than a person. They have argued that the phrase refers rather to the fact that the life of the Christian is controlled by Christ, both by His character as the Saviour who died and rose again to redeem us, and by His character as the Lord whose commands must determine our conduct. The truth probably lies in a combination of the two views. A believer is 'in Christ' by virtue of being united to Him by faith; and through such union with Him he shares in His saving power and comes under His sovereign authority. It is 'in Christ' that he is saved (Rom. 6: 23; 8: 1; 2 Cor. 5: 17), and as one who is 'in the Lord' he must obey His will (Col. 2: 6 f.; 1 Thes. 4: 1; 5: 12).[18]

Thus it may be said both that Christ is in believers and that they are in Him. The two complementary modes of expression indicate that He is united to His people so that here and now they may experience the fulness of His gifts to them. Their aim becomes to know Him and to be made like Him (Phil. 3: 10). As a result, Paul can speak of Christians forming a kind of 'corporate unity' with Christ. They form 'one body' composed of closely articulated members 'in Christ' (Rom. 12: 4 f.), and so close is their unity with Him that Paul can actually use the name 'Christ' to refer to Him and believers together (1 Cor. 12: 12).

The function of Jesus in this new relationship is that of 'head'. The title indicates His position of authority as Lord (Col. 1: 18; cf. 3: 15; Eph. 5: 23), but at the same time it means that He is the source of the spiritual life which flows through the body and nourishes the members (Eph. 3: 15 f.,; Col. 2: 19). The modern reader may smile at the curious physiology, but the spiritual truth expressed by it is not dependent on the literal truth of the metaphor. The important point is that believers form a united group, united to each other and to Christ who is their Lord and the source of their life.

'Christ in you' or 'you in Christ': the two phrases together indicate the character of the present work of Jesus in regard to His people. The latter, however, is Paul's predominant form of expression, and indicates that he thought of Christ as being a corporate personality, to whom the members of His church are joined by faith, and in whom He is active by His Spirit to save and to sanctify.

The Coming of Christ

We have already seen that the past work of Christ in His crucifixion and resurrection establishes the character of His work in the present and the future. As the One who rose from the dead, He now lives and gives His life to believers. Similarly, His resurrection is the

[18]Recent discussion is summarized in E. Best, *One Body in Christ* (1955) and J. K. S. Reid, *Our Life in Christ* (1963).

guarantee that He will raise His people from the dead and give them eternal salvation. It was the One whom God had raised from the dead who was expected to come from heaven, and whose coming formed the object of eager expectation by Paul and his early converts (1 Thes. 1: 10). The same hope burned equally brightly at the end of Paul's life, as we see from his exhortation to Timothy "by his appearing and his kingdom" (2 Tim. 4: 1).

Some scholars have suggested that Paul's thinking on this subject developed with the passage of time. At first, they say, Paul expected the coming of Jesus very soon; even 2 Thess. 2, with its reminder that certain other events must take place first, does not basically alter this hope. But as the years rolled on, Paul began to place less emphasis on the coming of Jesus to meet those who were still alive and to think more of the prospect of union with Christ after death. There is an element of truth in this hypothesis, but it can be greatly exaggerated. Throughout his life Paul looked forward to the appearing of Jesus, but as he grew older and faced the prospect of death (whether through illness or as a martyr) he began to reckon more seriously with the possibility that he, like some of the Thessalonian Christians, might fall asleep before that day. But whatever might happen to him, the vital point remained unaltered. For him life meant knowing Christ. If he died before Christ came, he would be brought into closer contact with Him and would in due course share in the resurrection at the coming of Christ. If he remained alive, he would await the coming of the Saviour from heaven. The juxtaposition of these two possibilities in the same letter (Phil. 1: 21–23; 3: 20) shows that there was no contradiction between them in Paul's mind. Not even death could separate the Christian from the love of Christ (Rom. 8: 35–39).[14]

The coming of Christ would mean judgement for those who had constituted themselves as His enemies, through their wilful ignorance of God or their disobedience to the Gospel (2 Thes. 1: 8). Jesus is consistently stated to be the One through whom God will carry out His judgement (Rom. 2: 16; 2 Cor. 5: 10; cf. Acts 17: 31), and it is probable that we should not attempt to distinguish between two separate acts of judgement, one by Christ and one by God; the close similarity in language between Rom. 14: 10 f. and 2 Cor. 5: 10 (cf. Phil. 2: 9–11) suggests that one event is meant, although the imagery used to describe it is varied. The wrath of God will be revealed

[14]Cf. F. F. Bruce in *Peake's Commentary* (1962), pp. 928–930.

against all unrighteousness, and the agent of judgement will be Christ.

But if His coming means judgement for the unbelieving, it means salvation for believers. Those who have already been justified by faith in Christ will be saved by Him from the wrath of God (Rom. 5: 9). For them the judgement cannot issue in condemnation, but rather in the gift of the crown of righteousness promised to all who look forward with loving anticipation to His appearing (2 Tim 4: 8).

It is not possible to construct a 'timetable' of the events associated with the coming of Christ from the teaching of Paul. It is sufficient for us to know that the coming of Christ is the moment for the resurrection of the dead and the conquest of evil. Then Christ hands over the sovereignty upon which He entered at His ascension to the Father, so that He may be all in all (1 Cor. 15: 20–28).

The Head of Creation

A Saviour who accomplishes the work described by Paul cannot be associated merely with the Church which He founded. Time and again the language of Paul shows that he could not think of Christ simply as the lord of the Church or of the individual Christian. The might and power of the Son of God could not be so delimited. For Paul He was the cosmic Christ, the Lord of creation. This means that Paul's conception of Christ's work stretches back far beyond His earthly appearance. If Christ was the Son of God sent into the world as its Saviour (Gal. 4: 4), then He existed before the foundation of the world and He created it. Before His incarnation He shared the divine glory (2 Cor. 8: 9) and the form of God (Phil. 2: 6). It was through Him that all things came into existence (1 Cor. 8: 6). Though the world did not recognize Him as such, He was its Creator, and though He is not recognized, yet it is through Him that the universe remains in being (Col. 1: 17). The climax of His work comes when all creation bows in submission before its Lord and gives Him the honour that is due to God (Phil. 2: 9–11).

That this is no late development of Paul's thought is seen from its appearance in so early an Epistle as 1 Cor. 8: 6. But for its fullest and finest expression we must turn to the hymn-like utterance in Col. 1: 13–20, which may fitly sum up the thought of Paul for us:[15]

[15]R. P. Martin, 'An Early Christian Hymn (Col. 1: 15-20)', *The Evangelical Quarterly* 36 (1964), pp. 195-205.

The Father . . . has delivered us from the dominion of darkness and transferred us into the kingdom of his beloved Son, in whom we have redemption, the forgiveness of sins.

He is the image of the invisible God, the first-born of all creation; for in him all things were created, in heaven and on earth, visible and invisible, whether thrones or dominions or principalities or authorities – all things were created through him and for him. He is before all things, and in him all things hold together.

He is the head of the body, the church; he is the beginning, the first-born from the dead, that in everything he might be pre-eminent. For in him all the fulness of God was pleased to dwell, and through him to reconcile to himself all things, whether on earth or in heaven, making peace by the blood of his cross.[16]

[16]Throughout the above chapter the Pastoral Epistles have been used as evidence for the mind of Paul, although it is a moot point whether they come directly from his pen or have been 'written up' by one of his friends.

Six

Priesthood and Sacrifice

A MONG THE NEW TESTAMENT WITNESSES TO THE WORK OF JESUS
the Epistle to the Hebrews is outstanding for the way in which
it adopts one particular category of interpretation and fully de-
velops its implications 'in depth' (as the current phrase puts it). We
cannot identify with any certainty either the author or his
readers, although there is a good case for seeing Apollos or his
spiritual twin in the former role. The writer was faced by a
situation in which a group of Christians were slipping back
from their faith in Christ. He responded to their backsliding with
this powerful homily, in which he states the finality of Jesus Christ
as God's last word to men (Heb. 1: 2).[1] He is the same, yesterday,
today and for ever (Heb. 13: 8), able to save for all time those
who come to God by Him (Heb. 7; 25), and apart from Him
there is no hope of salvation (Heb. 2: 3; cf. 3: 12–14; 6: 11 f.;
35–39).

It is not absolutely certain what was attracting the readers away
from their faith in Christ. They may have been slipping into a
nominal Christianity and failing to take their faith seriously, in the
manner of much modern apathetic religion, or they may have been
tempted towards Judaism, possibly because under its aegis they
would be free from the persecution that was coming upon them for
being Christians (Heb. 10: 32–34; 13: 3). Whatever be the truth
in these suggestions, the writer chose to depict the finality of Christ
for them by developing an extended contrast with the religious
system of the Old Testament and of Judaism. In doing so he paid
particular attention to one of the most fundamental aspects of that
religion, its system of priesthood and sacrifice.

In previous chapters we have already seen that the idea of the
death of Christ as a sacrifice was deep-rooted in the minds of the
early Christians. It was, for example, a fundamental concept in

[1] See F. F. Bruce, *The Apostolic Defence of the Gospel* (1959), pp. 78–86.

Paul's understanding of the cross. The writer to the Hebrews, how-ever, makes the fullest use of the theme, and in doing so he goes beyond his contemporaries in regarding Jesus Christ Himself as the high priest who offers the sacrifice. The concept of sacrifice is prone to the risk of being interpreted unsympathetically in sub-personal terms; the writer to the Hebrews avoids this danger by his insistence that Christ is both priest and sacrifice. He is the Mediator through whom a new covenant is established between God and men (Heb. 8: 6; 9: 15; 12: 24; cf. 1 Tim. 2: 5 f.).

The Superiority of Christ

The foundation of the writer's argument is that Christ is superior to all other possible intermediaries between God and man. He starts at the highest level by adducing scriptural evidence that Jesus has a status higher than that of the angels (Heb. 1–2). Contemporary Jewish documents show us the high esteem in which angels were held and indicate that some people even worshipped them. The writer to the Hebrews leaves his readers in no doubt that Christ is supreme. His statements show that he is thinking particularly of the status which Christ received at His exaltation (Heb. 1: 3b–4), but no more than Paul does he suggest that this status was some-thing new (Rom. 1: 3 f.; Phil. 2: 6–11). On the contrary, He makes it clear that Jesus was the eternal Son of God who shared the glory of God and bore the very stamp of His nature, and through whom God created the universe (Heb. 1: 2 f.). If for a time Jesus suffered humiliation and was made 'lower than the angels', this was for the special purpose of setting men free from death and sin. After His suffering He was reinstated in His former place, and now He sits at the right hand of God, worshipped and served by the angels. It is through this Son that God has spoken His word to men, and this message is of far higher importance than any communication ever conveyed to men by angels.

The message brought to men by the angels which the writer had in mind was not, of course, the Christmas message (e.g. Lk. 2: 8–15) but the law of Moses (cf. Gal. 3: 19). It is, therefore, not surprising that from the angels the writer turns to Moses, the human inter-mediary through whom God gave His covenant and law to Israel (Heb. 3: 1–4: 13). No man stood higher in Jewish estimation, but, as the writer points out, he had merely the rank of a servant in the household of God, whereas Jesus is the Son, supreme over the household. Once again the application is made: if men had to obey Moses under pain of God's wrath, how much more must they obey His Son.

The High Priest

So the writer proceeds with his comparisons, and next he places Jesus alongside the high priests of the Jewish religion (Heb. 4: 14–7: 28). As far as access to God was concerned, none occupied a more exalted position than the high priest, although even he could enter into the holiest part of the temple only once a year to appear before God for the people (Heb. 9: 7). He was called by God to officiate on behalf of men and also to minister to them by dealing "gently with the ignorant and wayward" (Heb. 5: 2).

Jesus, however, is superior to the earthly high priests of Israel. Like them He was appointed by God, but whereas Aaron's successors held their positions for a temporary period and were followed by their descendants, He continues for ever, and His priesthood has no end. Jewish priests were weak and sinful, like the people whom they represented, but Jesus was "holy, blameless, unstained, separated from sinners" (Heb. 7: 26). They had to offer sacrifices for their own sins before they could intercede for the people (Heb. 5: 3), but He had no need to do so.

As a result, it is the differences rather than the similarities between Jesus and the Jewish high priests which receive most emphasis. Indeed, the earthly analogue of Jesus is not to be found in the high priests of the tribe of Levi but in the priest-king Melchizedek. This enigmatic figure who appears briefly on the stage of history in the story of Abraham (Gen. 14: 18–20) was well suited to be a type of Christ. Nothing is said in Scripture about His parentage, birth or death, so that he is a reflection of Jesus who continues as a high priest for ever. Furthermore, Abraham, the forefather of the Levitical high priests, paid tithes to Melchizedek; since such a payment is always made by an inferior to a superior, it follows that the family from which Levi was to come was inferior to the priestly order of Melchizedek to which Christ was to belong.

This kind of argument may not appeal to modern readers in the same way as it would have done to Jewish Christians familiar with rabbinical methods of exegesis.[2] It should, therefore, be noted that the author's case does not rest upon this typology. His starting-point was Ps. 110: 4 where the messianic king is stated by a divine oath to be a priest like Melchizedek. In the light of this fact, the writer was able to see a number of resemblances between Melchizedek and Christ which he has here utilized to bring out the eternal and superior nature of Christ's priesthood. He is acting in the same way as a modern preacher who may develop various points in an analogy, for example, between leprosy and sin, not so much to *prove* what the characteristics of sin must be (an incurable disease leading to separation from God and ultimate death) as to *illustrate* them from something which is very similar.

At one point the earthly high priest may appear to be superior to Jesus. Jesus is presented as 'separated from sinners', but the earthly high priest is 'beset with weakness', and it might therefore be thought that the latter was better equipped to sympathize with sinners (Heb. 5: 2). This, however, is not the case. For here we must observe how careful the writer is to emphasize that Jesus became a man like us. He is fully conscious that a priest must be able to represent the people for whom he intercedes with God. Jesus was fitted to be a high priest not simply by being the Son of God appointed priest by a divine oath but also by being a man and undergoing human experiences. Like the other writers of New Testament Epistles, the author of Hebrews has not a great deal to say about the earthly life of Jesus, but what he does say is of great significance for the theme of priesthood. He tells us that Jesus was a real man, made of flesh (Heb. 5: 7), belonging to the tribe of Judah (Heb. 7: 14), who carried out a teaching ministry (Heb. 2: 3), and who suffered and died. Particular attention is given to the suffering and temptation of Jesus as the experiences which fitted Him to help those who are tempted (Heb. 2: 18). And lest we should be inclined to see an element of make-believe in these experiences, the writer uses the strongest possible language to indicate the reality of what Christ underwent. So great was the temptation that "he offered up prayers and supplications, with loud cries and tears, to him who was able to save him from death, and he was heard for

[2]The fact of Jewish speculation about Melchizedek in New Testament times has recently been demonstrated by the discovery in Cave 11 at Qumran of a fragmentary document in which he occupies a prominent role as a heavenly deliverer.

his godly fear" (Heb. 5: 7). The writer is conscious of the paradox inherent in his statement: "although he was a Son, he learned obedience through what he suffered" (Heb. 5: 8). In a way that we cannot fathom, Jesus as a man had to endure and be obedient to God; only in this way could He be 'perfect', a word which expresses the moral maturity and utter obedience that were required in the Saviour. Through His sufferings His entire dedication to God became apparent. As a man, Christ was fitted to be a high priest in every way.

Atonement and Covenant

Christ's experience of temptation prepared Him for His task as high priest. In common with the other New Testament authors the writer to the Hebrews sees the death and exaltation of Christ as the focal point of His work. His conception of Christ's work binds the death and the exaltation closely together as one great act of sacrifice. He is aware that the category of sacrifice is not fully adequate to express the meaning of Christ's death. Thus he understands the death of Jesus as a vicarious act in which He tasted death for every one (Heb. 2: 9). His meaning is plainly that Jesus died so that we need not taste the bitterness of death. For he goes on to describe how Jesus assumed human flesh and blood so that by dying as a man he might defeat the devil who has power over death (Heb. 2: 14). The association of the devil with death in this way is slightly unusual; the meaning appears to be that the devil attempts to deprive his victims of eternal life by enticing them to sin, accusing them before God, and so having them condemned to death as the result of their sin. By His death and resurrection Christ overcame death and entered heaven as the forerunner of believers (cf. Heb. 6: 20).

The writer's main thought, however, is that the death of Jesus was a sacrifice. As the true high priest He had to make an offering to God, and the offering which He made was Himself. Using the language of Ps. 40: 6–8, the writer speaks of Christ offering His body in sacrifice (Heb. 10: 5, 10, cf. 20). It should perhaps be noted that a real sacrifice is meant; on the basis of Heb. 10: 5 it has sometimes been thought that the obedience of Christ is contrasted with 'sacrifices and offerings', but the Epistle as a whole leaves no doubt that it was His actual death, obediently undergone, which constituted His saving act. This is confirmed by the way in which the writer, like Paul and Peter, lays stress on the shedding of Christ's blood (Heb. 9: 14). Under the old covenant forgiveness of sins was dependent upon the shedding of blood (Heb. 9: 22), and therefore it was necessary for Christ to shed His blood. In this way He removed the barrier of sin between God and men, an act variously described as making purification for sins (Heb. 1: 3), making propitiation for the sins of the people (Heb. 2: 17), and securing redemption (Heb. 9: 12). If the effects of the work of Christ are variously described in such terminology as this, so too the writer employs several types of Old Testament sacrifice as illustrations of the character of Christ's work. He draws a contrast between the outward cleansing of people defiled by contact with a dead body by means of the ashes of a sacrificial heifer (Num. 19: 9 f.) and the spiritual cleansing of the conscience by the blood of Christ (Heb. 9: 14). He pictures the death of Christ in terms of the sin offering which was burnt 'outside the camp' (Lev. 16: 27; Heb. 13: 11 f.). Two types of sacrifice in particular are described at length and they bring out the meaning of the death of Jesus with great effectiveness.

The first of these sacrifices is that of the Day of Atonement. Each year on the appointed day the high priest was required to offer an animal in sacrifice on the altar and then to sprinkle some of its blood on the 'mercy seat', the lid of the ark of the covenant, which was kept in the secrecy of the inmost part of the tabernacle. This was the vital point in the ceremonies of that day, on which the writer concentrates his attention; there were many other ceremonies associated with that day and indeed with the daily routine of the tabernacle, but, as our author himself says, "of these things we cannot now speak in detail". He is more concerned with the spiritual significance of the act. Since the tabernacle was constructed according to a heavenly pattern (Heb. 8: 5), he was able to understand the work of Christ in terms of an act of atonement performed in the true, heavenly sanctuary where God Himself is present and not simply a symbol of His presence (i.e. the ark of the covenant). What Christ did when He died and rose again was to enter that heavenly tabernacle into the very presence of God and there offer His own blood, shed on the cross, as an atonement for sin (Heb. 9: 11 f., 23 f., 10: 20).

Thus the death and ascension of Christ are seen to be a complete counterpart to the death of the sacrificial animal and the bringing

of its blood before God on the Day of Atonement. By this understanding of the work of Christ the writer has shown that the death
and ascension of Jesus belong inextricably together. They form the
two aspects of one saving event. Neither is complete without the
other. Furthermore, the writer has expressed with great clarity the
fact that the sacrifice of Christ was accepted by God the Father.
This was implicit in earlier New Testament writers who saw in the
resurrection of Jesus God's vindication of the work of His Son.
Here, however, for the first time we have an explicit indication of
the way in which the sacrifice of Christ was offered to God and
accepted by Him. The divine seal is set upon the work of Christ.

Another deduction made by the writer is of the utmost importance. He draws a contrast between the repeated, annual acts of
sacrifice carried out by the earthly high priests and the one act of
sacrificial offering performed by Christ. He did not have to offer
Himself repeatedly; He has appeared once for all to put away sin by
the sacrifice of Himself (Heb. 9: 25 f.). Christ's death is a *once-for-
all* act. What is even more important is that it is a *finished* act.
When Christ had made His offering, He sat down at the right hand
of God (Heb. 1: 3; 8: 1; 12: 2). The writer interprets this fact to mean
that the sacrificial work of Christ is finished and complete. It is not
simply that His death took place once-for-all; His offering of Himself to God in the heavenly sanctuary also took place once-for-all.
"When Christ had offered for all time a single sacrifice for sins, he
sat down at the right hand of God, then to wait until his enemies
should be made a stool for his feet. For by a single offering he has
perfected for all time those who are sanctified" (Heb. 10: 12–14).
There is, therefore, no need for any repetition of His sacrifice or any
re-representation of it to God; to make any such suggestion is to
call in question the perfection and completion of "the finished work
of Christ".[3]

Hence, our privilege and responsibility is simply to enter into the
presence of God in the name of Christ. We can draw near to the
throne of divine grace with confidence because Christ has opened
up a new and living way for us; the veil separating God from his
people has been removed (cf. Mk. 15: 38).

The second Old Testament sacrifice which is fulfilled and trans-
cended in Christ is that associated with the covenant. The covenant
was the agreement offered by God to the people of Israel in which

[3]Cf. A. M. Stibbs, *The Finished Work of Christ* (1954).

He pledged Himself to care for them and imposed upon them the obligations of worshipping Him and keeping His law. It was inaugurated by a sacrifice (Ex. 24). After the people had rejected their obligations and come under God's judgement for their faithlessness, He graciously offered to them a new covenant under which they would be forgiven and have God's law written on their hearts (Jer. 31: 31–34). The writer to the Hebrews takes up this prophecy (cf. Mk. 14: 24) and finds in it the justification for the priestly activity of Christ. Under the old covenant made with Moses there was a priesthood from the tribe of Levi in which Christ had no part. But the new covenant required a new priesthood, and Christ is seen to be its high priest. The promise of a new covenant included the gracious affirmation of God that He would be merciful to the iniquities of His people and remember their sins no more (Heb. 8: 12). Such an act of forgiveness required an act of sacrifice, similar to that which inaugurated the old covenant at Sinai. The writer takes advantage of the double meaning of the Greek word used in the Septuagint for 'covenant' (*diatheke*). In secular Greek it meant 'will' or 'testament', and since a will becomes effective only upon the death of the testator, so the new covenant promised by Jeremiah became effective only upon the death of Christ, the mediator (Heb. 9: 15–18). The death of Christ is therefore seen as corresponding to the inaugural sacrifice of the old covenant. With the sacrificial blood Moses had sprinkled the people and the various utensils of their worship in order that they might be purified and acceptable to God. In the same way, believers are sprinkled with the blood of Christ in order that their consciences and hearts may be cleansed and they may be acceptable to God (Heb. 9: 14; 10: 22, 29; 12: 24; 13: 20).

If the imagery of the Day of Atonement spoke of an offering made to God, that of the covenant sacrifice speaks of a cleansing of God's people. Both ways of speaking express the same reality, namely that through the sacrificial death of Christ atonement is made for human sin. God is reconciled to sinners,[4] and they become acceptable in His sight.

From now on the old covenant is obsolete. Its sacrifices could not really take away sin (Heb. 9: 9; 10: 4), for they were purely external. The Old Testament itself recognized that something inward

[4]For a justification of this way of expressing the matter (which is admittedly not found in so many words in the Bible) see L. Morris, *The Apostolic Preaching of the Cross* (1955), ch. 6.

G

and spiritual was required (e.g. Ps. 51: 16 f.), and the sacrificial system was meant to be an outward symbol of a spiritual offering. Now through the offering of Christ sins committed under the old covenant are forgiven (Heb. 9: 15). The old covenant has become obsolete; the superiority and finality of the new is beyond question (Heb. 8: 13).

The Perfecter of Our Faith

The particular purpose of the writer to the Hebrews led him to concentrate his attention on the work of Christ as He offered the final, perfect sacrifice for the sins of men. For Christians to turn aside from the message of that sacrifice was to commit apostasy from their faith (Heb. 10: 29). The writer had, therefore, to encourage his readers to remain steadfast in their allegiance to Christ, and he did this particularly by means of his teaching on the need for a constant faith which perseveres to the end against every temptation. Although his stress falls largely on the need for such faith, he does not ignore the significance of the present work of Jesus for His tempted people

Although Christ's work of offering sacrifice lay in the past, His work as a high priest was not finished. Seated at the right hand of God, He still retains that status and office. His work now is to help those who are tempted (Heb. 2: 18; 4: 14–16). In this connection great importance is attached to His heavenly intercession for His people. As the One who has entered heaven on their behalf, He continues in His priestly office by making intercession for them. When they draw near to God in prayer, they may be sure that He will receive them and answer their petition (Heb. 7: 24 f.). The presence of Christ, who was made man and suffered temptation Himself, assures them that they will be heard sympathetically (Heb. 4: 14–16).

At the same time the writer probably also thinks of Christ as working in the lives of His people. To be sure, this thought is not developed at great length. But when the writer speaks of God working in believers and equipping them to do His will "through Jesus Christ", it is clear that he does not regard Jesus as helping His people only from a heavenly throne (Heb. 13: 21). The way in which he describes Him as "the great shepherd of the sheep" confirms this impression (Heb. 13: 20). Jesus is further presented as an example for believers to imitate when they undergo temptation and tribulation. As they run in the race of the Christian life, watched by those who have already fulfilled their course, they are to look towards Jesus Himself who was prepared to endure the cross and its shame before entering into the joy of heaven (Heb. 12: 1 f.). But Jesus here is more than an example. He is "the pioneer and perfecter of our faith", a phrase which probably means not merely that He Himself is the example of a perfect faith but also that He perfects the faith of His followers. He calls them to fresh endeavours, and as they look to Him they receive strength and succour to persevere to the end.

So they run their race, their eyes fixed on Him. Before them is the promise that He will come again for those who are eagerly waiting for Him (Heb. 9: 28; 10: 37). This time, however, He comes not in humiliation to offer sacrifice for sin, but in glory. His coming is associated with the day of God's final judgement upon sin, and the thought is inescapable that the Christ who died to cleanse His people from sin will be with them on the day of judgement, welcoming them into the presence of God where He already sits as a forerunner on their behalf (Heb. 6: 20).

Seven

Revelation and Victory

IN ONE OF HIS BOOKS THE LATE W. F. HOWARD JUXTAPOSED THE
words of two hymns which express different types of religion.
The first was:

> Open, Lord, my inward ear,
>   And bid my heart rejoice;
> Bid my quiet spirit hear
>   Thy comfortable voice;
> Never in the whirlwind found,
>   Or where earthquakes rock the place,
> Still and silent is the sound,
>   The whisper of Thy grace.

The second was:

> Come, Thou Conqueror of the nations,
>   Now on Thy white horse appear;
> Earthquakes, dearths and desolations
>   Signify Thy kingdom near;
> True and faithful!
> 'Stablish Thy dominion here.

Of the first Howard said, "That is the prayer of a Christian mystic";
and of the second, "That is the dialect of undiluted Jewish apocalyptic."[1] Yet, as he went on to show, both come from the pen of
one writer, Charles Wesley, and they are dated respectively in 1742
and 1759.

The point which Howard wished to illustrate with this example
was the combination of mysticism and eschatology in the teaching
of Jesus. For our present purpose, however, we may use the analogy
as some justification for daring to treat together in one single chapter such apparently diverse approaches to the work of Jesus as those
of the Gospel and First Epistle of John, on the one hand, and the

[1]W. F. Howard, *Christianity according to St John* (1943), pp. 201–204.

Revelation of John, on the other. (We may pass over 2 and 3 John which make no important contribution to our theme.) At first sight, the two sets of writings are so divergent in outlook that it is difficult to believe that they come from the same author or the same literary environment.[2] The example of Charles Wesley shows that such apparently divergent outlooks can – and indeed must – be combined if we are to do justice to the New Testament and to attain to a mature understanding of Christian theology. In fact the two approaches converge at a significant point. In the Gospel and Epistle the past coming of Jesus is evaluated in terms of its importance for the present life of the Christian; in the Revelation Christians suffering persecution have their minds directed to the future work of Jesus, a work whose content and character is again understood from His past work. In each case, it is Jesus who is at the centre of the writer's thought, and it is His earthly work which is of decisive importance.

Revelation and Salvation

The First Epistle of John is not especially concerned with the work of Jesus as such. The situation which confronted the author was that false beliefs about the person of Christ were threatening the Church. At the same time those who promulgated these views were falling short of the ethical standards characteristic of true faith in Christ. The primary task of John, therefore, was to reaffirm that Jesus was truly the Christ, the Son of God, and to demonstrate that the true Christian is distinguished by his faith, love and freedom from sin. He lays particular stress on the fact that the Son of God was truly incarnate in Jesus Christ (1 Jn. 5: 6 refers to the reality of His baptism and His death), but a developed statement of the work of Jesus was less germane to his purpose. For an understanding of the work of Jesus we must supplement the teaching of the Epistle from the Gospel; earlier we made use of its contents in our study of Jesus' own concept of His work, but it is equally appropriate to use it now for the evidence which it affords regarding the theology of John himself.

The Epistle begins by speaking of the revelation of 'life' which was given to men in the historical appearance of Jesus Christ on

[2]On the problem of the authorship of the Johannine literature see J. D. Douglas (ed.), *The New Bible Dictionary* (1962), pp. 644 f.

earth (1 Jn. 1: 1 f.). Elsewhere John tells us that eternal life consists in knowing God and Jesus Christ whom He sent (Jn. 17: 3). A combination of the two passages suggests that for John the purpose of the coming of Jesus was to reveal God to men so that by accepting the revelation they might have eternal life. To believe that Jesus is the Christ, the Son of God, is the key to the possession of life (Jn. 20: 31). In Christ God is revealed to men. "The Son of God has come to give us understanding, to know him who is true" (1 Jn. 5: 20).

This impression that the work of Jesus is to reveal God is confirmed by the prologue to the Gospel, which gives us the author's own summary of the meaning of the incarnation. Jesus is here identified with the eternal, pre-existent Word through whom God the Father created the universe. By calling Jesus 'the Word' John means that He is the agent of God's self-revelation to men. Through the knowledge of God which He bestows men receive life and light. The light is the light of divine revelation which shines in the darkness of a sinful world, and it is specifically said to be the source of life for them (Jn. 1: 4). The content of the revelation is God Himself (Jn. 1: 18), whose grace and truth are revealed in His Son (Jn. 1: 17).

From this evidence we may conclude that John regarded the work of Jesus as being to reveal the Father, who is the source of eternal life, to men. Our earlier study of the ministry of Jesus has shown that He did claim to do precisely this. He revealed to men that God called them into a filial relationship with Himself, and in His own actions and words He acted as God acts so that those who saw Him truly saw God. The Gospel of John as a whole confirms this interpretation of the work of Jesus. When Jesus Himself summed up His work in His great prayer to God, He stated: "I glorified thee on earth, having accomplished the work which thou gavest me to do . . . I have manifested thy name . . . I have given them the words which thou gavest me . . ." (Jn. 17: 4–8). The work of Jesus, as described by John, consisted of signs and sayings. The purpose of the signs was to reveal the divine glory of Jesus (Jn. 2: 11), and in His discourses He declared that He was the revealer of God. In His great sayings, each beginning with the words 'I am', He laid claim to being the source of those divine gifts which bring spiritual life to men, and He invited people to believe in Him, that is to say, to receive Him and thus become sons of God (Jn. 1: 12).

In His other teaching He put before them the words of God, and in particular the great command that they should love each other; He Himself was the example of what this meant in practice (Jn. 13: 15). The whole intent of His ministry was to show that He was in the Father and the Father in Him, a form of phrase which indicates the closeness of the union between the unseen Father and the Son who manifests Him to the world (Jn. 10: 38). His death upon the cross was the supreme proof of the love of God (1 Jn. 3: 16; 4: 9; Jn. 3: 16) and of the fact that Jesus was the Son of God (Jn. 8: 28), for in it His glory was revealed.

All of this might well suggest that John regarded Jesus as being the Saviour of the world *simply* because He revealed God to men. All that He required men to do in order to receive eternal life was to accept Him as the accredited Messenger of God (Jn. 6: 29). He came to show men how to worship God in spirit and in truth (Jn. 4: 24–26). All that men need to do is to receive Him (Jn. 1: 12) and to keep His words (Jn. 8: 51). To believe that Jesus is the Son of God saves a man from death (Jn. 8: 24) and brings him the assurance that God will raise him up at the last day (Jn. 6: 40). Thus it is the truth revealed in Christ which sets men free from their present existence (Jn. 8: 32) and brings them into the sphere where they may know and see God. And after Christ has returned to be with His Father, the Holy Spirit continues to perform the same tasks of opening the eyes of men to their need and revealing God in Christ to them (Jn. 14: 26; 16: 7–15).

Revelation and Reconciliation

This understanding of John's teaching about Christ as the revealer of God is of great importance. It fits in, as we have seen, with Jesus' own concept of His work. It is confirmed by the evidence of Paul who tells us that God "has shone in our hearts to give the light of the knowledge of the glory of God in the face of Christ" (2 Cor. 4: 6), a sentence that could almost have been written by John. Consequently, it has appeared to many writers that this category of 'revelation' sums up the thought of John regarding the work of Jesus.

We may well agree with this verdict. If we want an overall term to describe John's view of the work of Christ, then 'revelation' is as good as any. Where, however, we must dissociate ourselves from advocates of this interpretation of John is when they go on to claim that John's concept of revelation is completely summed up in the evidence which we have just cited (admittedly and necessarily in a selective manner). The attentive reader will be well aware that there is still much to be said if we are to gain a balanced picture of John's teaching. What we must in fact ask is whether Jesus *does* anything or needs to *do* anything in order that men may have eternal life. Did John consider it sufficient that He had simply revealed God to men? Is it enough that Jesus simply presented Himself to men as the Son of God and challenged them to decision?

The answer to these rhetorical questions must undoubtedly be 'No'. We may agree with A. M. Hunter when he writes, "Certainly Paul is more at home in the category of reconciliation, as John is in that of revelation. But let us beware of drawing this contrast too sharply."[8] The truth of the matter is that for John the revelation of God in Christ has as its essential ingredient the revelation of His reconciling love. And this revelation is not simply a display of the loving character of God, but rather a manifestation of His gracious act in dealing with the sins of men. For John, every bit as much as for the other New Testament writers, men are sinners, guilty in God's sight, in need of cleansing, and unable to deliver themselves. Their need is not some kind of spiritual illumination, not even simply a new birth which will bring them into a new sphere of life, but an act of God which will atone for their sin and cleanse them from its defilement. The revelation which is given to us in John is the revelation that the man Jesus Christ is the Saviour of the world because His death on the cross is God's saving act for mankind.

Turning to the Epistle, which, as we have already observed, is not primarily concerned to delineate the character of the work of Christ, we find that the common, apostolic teaching about the death of Christ is clearly and unequivocally expressed. At the very outset we are reminded that the blood of Christ cleanses us from all sin (1 Jn. 1: 7). There is no need to delay over the meaning of the phrase, for we are at once brought into the sphere of the sacrificial language and the ideas of cleansing which are typical of Peter and the writer to the Hebrews. Likewise, John tells us that Jesus Christ

---

[8]*Introducing New Testament Theology*, p. 131. 'Reconciliation' in this quotation should not be understood too narrowly as a technical term; Paul's general application of the ideas of atonement and propitiation to the death of Jesus is in mind.

is the propitiation for the sins of the whole world (1 Jn. 2: 2), and we owe to Him the magnificent statement of the character of God's love: "In this is love, not that we loved God but that He loved us and sent his Son to be the propitiation for our sins" (1 Jn. 4: 10). The best comment remains the classic words of James Denney.

So far from finding any kind of contrast between love and propitiation, the apostle can convey no idea of love to anyone except by pointing to the propitiation – love is what is manifested there; and he can give no account of the propitiation but by saying, "Behold what manner of love." For him, to say "God is love" is exactly the same as to say, "God has in His Son made atonement for the sin of the world." If the propitiatory death of Jesus is eliminated from the love of God, it might be unfair to say that the love of God is robbed of all meaning, but it is certainly robbed of its apostolic meaning. It has no longer that meaning which goes deeper than sin, sorrow, and death, and which recreates life in the adoring joy, wonder and purity of the first Epistle of John.[4]

The main thrust of the Epistle is thus that the death of Jesus was sacrificial in character. If this were not enough to demonstrate that for John the revelatory character of the death of Jesus lies in its quality as a deed, we may add to the evidence the fact that John also sees the work of Christ as a conflict with the devil. The reason why the Son of God was manifested was to destroy the works of the devil (1 Jn. 3: 8).

All this finds a sure basis in the teaching of the Gospel. There Jesus is given such titles as 'Messiah' and 'Son of man' which traditionally pointed to someone who was to *act* as God's representative rather than merely to *be* an example or illustration of His character. He spoke of the 'work' which He had to do, and the dynamic words used to explicate this phrase suggest that something active and positive is meant (cf. Jn. 5: 17 ff.). Above all we find that the death of Jesus is given that same significance which it has elsewhere in the New Testament. The tone of the Gospel is set at the very outset by John's description of Jesus as the Lamb of God who takes away the sin of the world (Jn. 1: 29, 36; cf. 1 Jn. 3: 5). We are undoubtedly meant to see a prophecy of the death of Christ, that act which was for Jesus Himself the culmination of His ministry. He

[4]*The Death of Christ*, p. 152.

saw it as being like the death of a seed, the inevitable precondition for the production of much fruit (Jn. 12: 24).

Those who know nothing else about the Gospel of John may know that one verse crystallizes its message: "God so loved the world that he gave his only Son, that whoever believes in him should not perish but have eternal life" (Jn. 3: 16). The way in which this verse is preceded by a reference to the Son of man being 'lifted up', like the bronze serpent in the wilderness, leaves us in no doubt that the divine 'giving' of Jesus was a 'giving' of Him to death so that we might live. Moreover, this death, the token of divine grace, was a sacrificial act for the benefit of mankind. One recent writer has affirmed that John never ascribes a saving efficacy to the cross or says that Christ died 'for us'.[5] The statement is patently false, for nothing could be clearer than the twice-repeated saying that the good shepherd lays down his life *for the sheep* (Jn. 10: 11, 15). Precisely the same meaning is to be found in the statement, 'Greater love has no man than this, that a man lay down his life for his friends." In itself it is a general statement, capable of being inscribed on a war memorial or in some other context of human self-sacrifice. But just as Paul, after making a very similar statement, goes on to describe the greater act of love shown by God in Christ (Rom. 5: 7 f.), so too in John the general statement is immediately followed by the word of Jesus, "You are my friends" (Jn. 15: 13 f.). It should require little competence in logic to draw the implied conclusion. If further evidence be required, it is given by the words of Caiaphas, "one man should die for the people", in which the Evangelist sees expressed the deeper thought that "Jesus should die for the nation, and . . . to gather into one the children of God who are scattered abroad" (Jn. 11: 50–52). Finally, the way in which it is said that men may have life through eating the flesh of Christ and drinking His blood (Jn. 6: 53 f.) unmistakably suggests that men receive life through the benefits of Christ's passion and death; the language is reminiscent of the words of Jesus at the Last Supper and implies that life is made available only through the death of Jesus (cf. also Jn. 17: 19 where Jesus consecrates Himself to His impending death for the sake of the disciples).

Not much is said in the Epistle and Gospel of John about the significance of the resurrection and ascension as aspects of the work of Christ. John views the cross so much in the light of the resurrec-

[5]S. Schulz, *Die Stunde der Botschaft* (1967), p. 306.

tion that he is able to speak of the death of Christ as being itself the glorification of Christ (Jn. 12: 23). The cross itself, as a place of lowly service, is a revelation of the glory of God. The death and resurrection of Jesus together constitute the act in which the present evil world is judged, its prince cast out, and men are enabled to come and find eternal life (Jn. 12: 31 f.). For John the significance of the resurrection is that it prepares the way for a continuing work of Christ after His earthly ministry.

Christ and His Church

If Jesus were merely the revealer of the character of God, there would be no place for the continuing, heavenly work which is described at length in the writings of John. Christ is presented, first, as the Advocate who intercedes for believers with the Father (1 Jn. 2: 1). In his Epistle, John presented his readers with the plain ideal that Christians ought to be free from sin; to sin is a denial of the true character of one who abides in Christ (1 Jn. 3: 6, 9). But the pastor who had to put this ideal firmly before those who were morally indifferent knew well that the believer who seeks most zealously to fulfil this ideal can still fall into sin; to say that we have no sin is both foolish and false. This, however, is no reason to give up the battle or to despair of forgiveness for sin often repeated. Jesus Christ, who died for the sins of the world, continues to act as heavenly intercessor for the sinful, and they are assured of pardon and entry into divine fellowship. Nor does His activity confine itself to this one fundamental matter. When believers pray to the Father in the name of Christ they are assured of an answer to their prayers (Jn. 15: 16; 16: 23; cf. 14: 13 f.). By themselves these verses might suggest that the Father hears us only because the Son induces Him to do so. That this is not the case is clearly shown by other texts which indicate that the Father readily hears the prayers of His children (Jn. 16: 26 f.; 1 Jn. 3: 21 f.; 5: 14 f.). The purpose of the picture of Christ as a heavenly intercessor is to help those who know Christ but have not seen the Father; it assures them that God will hear their prayers through Christ.

As in Paul the work of Christ for us is matched by His work in union with us, so too in John the thought of Christ's continuing work in His people is of supreme importance. Christ presents Himself as the good shepherd who cares for His sheep, and it is probable that He was thinking of His future relationship to His followers, especially when He spoke of the 'other sheep' who were to form part of His flock (Jn. 10: 16). He cares for His sheep and keeps them from the attacks of the evil one (1 Jn. 5: 18). But alongside this somewhat external relationship there is the fact of a close spiritual union between Christ and His disciples. Believers abide in Christ (Jn. 15: 4–10; 1 Jn. 2: 24, 28; 3: 6), and at the same time He abides in them (Jn. 15: 4 f.). They are joined to Him as branches are to the stem of a vine, so that they are 'in Him', and His life flows to the branches so that He is 'in them'. This mutual relationship is similar to that which exists between the Father and the Son (Jn. 14: 10).

What is said of the relationship between Christ and His disciples is also said of the relationship between the Father and men (Jn. 14: 23; 17: 21; 1 Jn. 4: 4; 5: 20). It is also true of the Holy Spirit. Jesus promised that He would send the Holy Spirit to abide in His disciples after his glorification (Jn. 1: 33, 7: 39; cf. 1 Jn. 2: 20, 27). He would be 'another Comforter' and would take the place of the earthly Jesus in the experience of the disciples (Jn. 14: 16, 26; 15: 26; 16: 7–15). He would abide in believers (Jn. 14: 17).

These references (which are not fully listed) show that the presence of God – Father, Son and Spirit – is with Christians. They are lifted up into an experience of eternal life, which consists in knowing God. The life of Jesus has made the Father known to them, and Jesus' own gift of the Spirit continues the revelation to His disciples. Thus, as in Paul, we have paradoxical but complementary expressions about the relationship of believers to God which attempt to put into stammering words the reality of the eternal life given by God to men. The experience is greater than the language and constantly bursts its barriers.

For John this present experience of Christ is the main theme of his theology. It is an experience which at all points is determined by the revelation of God given in the earthly ministry of Christ. Those who had seen Him in the days of His flesh bore their testimony in order that another generation might enter into fellowship with the Father and the Son (Jn. 1: 14; 1 Jn. 1: 1–4). But John, like Peter, was fully aware that believers walk by faith and not by sight (Jn. 20: 29; cf. 1 Jn. 3: 2). Although, therefore, more than any other New Testament writer he emphasizes that 'Tomorrow is now' (the phrase is Neville Clark's),[6] that the last judgement already takes

[6] N. Clark, *Interpreting the Resurrection* (1967), ch. 3.

place when men encounter Christ, and that the eternal life of heaven is already given to men in Christ (e.g. Jn. 3: 18, 36; 5: 25), yet for him the Christian life is a life of hope, centred on the coming of Christ. He will be the judge of all men at the last day (Jn. 5: 25–29), and will raise up His people to eternal life (Jn. 6: 35, 39 f., 44, 54; 11: 24–26). For those whom He raises from the dead and those who may live until His coming (Jn. 21: 22 f.) He is already preparing a heavenly future, and He will come for them to take them to be with Himself (Jn. 14: 3). They will see and share in His glory (Jn. 17: 3), and as they see Him, so they will be made like Him, righteous and pure (1 Jn. 2: 28–3: 3). The Christ who came to reveal the Father to them, whom they know in personal communion, is the object of their faith and of their hope.

The Lord of the Church

In turning from the Gospel and Epistle of John to the Revelation, one is strongly tempted to adopt this hope of the coming of Christ as the starting-point of the exposition. With its constant refrain that the Lord is coming (Rev. 1: 7 and 22: 20 frame the contents of the book), it may well seem that the Revelation takes up the final coming of Christ and makes it its chief theme. But while this is a correct insight, we shall find that in fact John begins from the historic fact of Christ's death and resurrection, so that we too must adopt this as our starting-point.

The presentation of Christian truth demands that an expositor must take account of the varying circumstances of his audience and show how the essential message of God in Christ is relevant to their needs. The considerable differences between the various Johannine writings are an illustration of this point. The Gospel has an evangelistic purpose, although it goes beyond the requirements of an evangelistic tract by showing the importance of the work of Christ for the Christian life, and it hints at the possibility of persecution for His followers (Jn. 15: 18–16: 4). The First Epistle confronts the rise of heresy about the person of Christ and ethical indifference in the Church. The Revelation is addressed to a situation in which persecution had become a grim reality (Rev. 2: 13) for the Church. John had to deal with two matters in facing this situation. First, he had to strengthen a Church that had lost its first love for its Lord; the weak had to be encouraged to bear a steadfast witness, and those who were trifling with sin had to be warned of the spiritual danger in which they stood. Second, he had to assure the Church that its tribulations would end in final victory; a heavenly plan was being worked out, and ultimately evil would be destroyed and the kingship of God openly established. The message which Jesus Christ gave to John in this situation was that He is the Lord of the Church and of all human history.

To say that Jesus was Lord, especially in a world which knew "many 'gods' and many 'lords'" (1 Cor. 8: 5 f.), was to run the risk of conforming Christ to a misleading pattern. Even to speak of Him in biblical language as "the Lion of the tribe of Judah, the root of David" (Rev. 5: 5) could cause a false impression. From the outset, therefore, the Revelation uses words like grace and peace (Rev. 1: 4) and presents Christ as the One who loves His people and has freed them from their sins by his blood (Rev. 1: 5). As in 1 Jn. 4: 10, so here the proof and essence of the divine love for man is seen in the death of Christ which frees men from sin. The familiar imagery of ransom appears in the song of praise in heaven: "Worthy art thou to take the scroll and to open its seals, for thou wast slain and by thy blood didst ransom men for God from every tribe and tongue and people and nation, and hast made them a kingdom and priests to our God, and they shall reign on earth" (Rev. 5: 9 f.). These words are addressed to Christ who appears in the guise of a Lamb (Rev. 5: 6). It is, therefore, sacrificial blood which is the ransom price for men, and the same blood is the means by which men are cleansed from their sin; in the language of Revelation "they have washed their robes and made them white in the blood of the Lamb" (Rev. 7: 14; 22: 14).

Although the figure of the Lamb is purely sacrificial in the rest of the New Testament, it is here also a symbol of authority, perhaps as the leader of the flock.[7] The Lamb which had been slain but had been raised from the dead is Jesus who was triumphant in His endurance of the cross and was raised from the dead. He is the first-born from the dead, and He enjoys the privileges of supremacy which are associated with the first-born in a family (Rev. 1: 5). Thus His victory at the cross entitles Him to be the Lord of the Church.

This is apparent from the opening scene in the book. Jesus is here given the title of Son of man, which in itself betokens supremacy,

[7] C. H. Dodd, *The Interpretation of the Fourth Gospel* (1953), pp. 231 f.

and He is described as having the accoutrements of the Ancient of Days in the vision of Daniel. In this supreme, indeed divine, role He is seen standing in the midst of the seven lampstands which symbolize the various congregations in His Church. He addresses royal commands to them. He threatens judgement upon the faithless and sinful, and He promises the highest rewards to those who conquer, that is to say, who endure faithfully to the end. As the Lord of the Church, He cares for the Church. This is indicated by the way in which He stands among the lampstands and holds in His hand the seven stars which represent the angels of the Churches. Above all, He promises His personal presence and fellowship to those who hear Him knocking at the door and give Him entrance. The promise that He will eat with His disciples (Rev. 3: 20) irresistibly suggests a reference to His spiritual presence in the Lord's Supper. Although some scholars have held that His promise is addressed to the Church as a whole there ought not to be any doubt that He is speaking graciously to each and every individual in the Church and offering to come to them. The traditional evangelistic use of the text is fully justified.[8]

The future hopes of the Church are pinned upon the coming of Christ to take His people to be with Himself and to resurrect those who have died, especially as martyrs for the faith (Rev. 20: 4). A variety of pictures are used to bring out the richness of that experience of communion which they will enjoy when they see Him. They will dwell in the new Jerusalem, the heavenly city (Rev. 21: 10 ff.). By a swift transition of metaphor the city is described as the bride of the Lamb (Rev. 21: 2), and the saints are invited to the marriage supper (Rev. 19: 7–9). Since elsewhere in the New Testament the people of God are described as forming a temple or a building (Eph. 2: 20–22; 1 Pet. 2: 5) or as being the bride of Christ (Eph. 5: 22–33), we should not take John's language to mean that Christ's followers are merely guests or spectators at the wedding; the thought is surely that they are brought into the closest fellowship with Him. There is no temple in the heavenly city because God and the Lamb are personally present. The Lamb's servants see His face, and His name is written upon them as a sign that they belong to Him. He cares for them, as a Shepherd cares for his sheep (Rev. 7: 17), and gives them the water of life. In heaven Christ is to His disciples all that He was to them on earth and all that He is to them

[8]So, for example, W. Hendriksen, *More than Conquerors* (1962), pp. 77–79.

now. His work is to love them, and this He does throughout
eternity. Until that day when they will enter into the fulness of
eternal life they treasure His promise, "Surely I am coming soon",
and pray "Amen. Come, Lord Jesus" (Rev. 21: 20).

The Lord of History

But what assurance is there that He will come? In a world of persecution and tribulation, where Satan is enthroned (cf. Rev. 2: 13),
men may well be tempted to reject the hope as sheer illusion. The
answer given by John is the same as that found in the rest of the
New Testament.[9] Jesus Christ is Lord, not only of the Church which
He purchased with His blood and whose members freely yield Him
their allegiance, but also of the whole universe and its history. The
Lamb is a victorious Lamb, and under His leadership His people will
triumph. Having received power from His Father, He conquered by
patiently enduring the cross (Rev. 2: 27; 3: 21) and He promises a
share in His rule to His disciples. The first-born from the dead is
mightier than death and the devil. The devil has already been overcome (Rev. 12: 10), and those who follow in the footsteps of Christ
will conquer him also (Rev. 12: 11). The devil's power is limited; he
is like a dog straining at his leash.

Consequently, the process of history is under God's control. The
vision of the future granted to John was contained in a sealed book,
the opening of which was the signal for its programme to commence. Only one person was worthy to open the book, the Lamb
of God, and He was worthy because He had been *slain*. What is now
unfolded in history is the judgement of God upon a sinful world.
The forces of evil resist to the last ditch and take a heavy toll of
God's people, but their doom is certain. They are conquered by the
steadfastness of the saints who love not their lives unto death.

The end comes when Christ reappears at the head of the heavenly
armies, and the last battle takes place (Rev. 19: 11–16). Many com-
mentators have taken the language of battle quite literally – or at
least the *fact* of battle, since the description of a cavalry regiment
belongs to the tactics of a past age. But, as some recent scholars
have observed,[10] it is incredible that after Christ's followers have

[9]For a full-scale exposition of the hope of Christ's coming see A. L. Moore,
The Parousia in the New Testament (1966).

[10]I owe this insight to a lecture by Prof. F. F. Bruce. It is carried too far by
G. B. Caird, *The Revelation of St John the Divine* (1966).

conquered by the word of their testimony and by the blood of the Lamb (i.e. readiness for martyrdom), they should now take up arms for offensive warfare. In fact no battle is described, only its issue. Armageddon is a symbol for the final defeat of evil by the power of Christ.

Then comes the promised end. The defeat of evil is followed by its judgement. The wrath of the Lamb (Rev. 6: 16) is finally revealed. God's implacable opposition to evil is displayed, and all those who have yielded their souls to evil suffer the ultimate judgement of God. Then the kingdoms of the world will acknowledge their rightful Lord, and Christ and His saints reign for ever and ever. The process of history has reached its promised climax, and Christ is the divine agent through whom God's purpose comes to fulfilment.

Eight

Christt and Us

I N THE PRECEDING PAGES AN ATTEMPT HAS BEEN MADE TO SET OUT
the teaching of the New Testament on the work of Christ in its
own words and with the minimum of explanation. It is inevitable
that in such an exposition an author sees things from his own
particular point of view; he selects from the New Testament those
things which in his judgement were important for the original
writers, and he expounds them from the position of a twentieth-
century interpreter who is heir to the tradition of scholarship and
exposition of the Christian Church (however much or little of these
rich resources he may have used). Nevertheless, allowing for these
subjective elements which colour every attempt to understand
what somebody else has said or written, we hope that this book has
some claim to represent accurately what the New Testament
writers actually said.

Certain features of the New Testament doctrine of the work of
Jesus should have become apparent. The first of them is that there
is a definite unity in the theology of the New Testament.[1] We have
discovered that a whole series of writers nurtured in different back-
grounds and addressing themselves to different situations have an
essentially common understanding of the work of Jesus. They see
that the central element in the Christian message is the death and
resurrection of Jesus; in this great event God acted to save men
from their sins. The same categories of interpretation keep re-
curring; the themes of sacrifice, redemption, victory and revelation
are constantly to be found. The work of Christ is inspired by divine
grace and its result is the benefit of mankind. Likewise, in varying
degrees all the writers emphasize that the work of Christ is not
confined to His earthly ministry and His resurrection. They look
back to the creation of the universe and see Christ active there as

[1]This was the conclusion of J. Denney, *The Death of Christ*, p. 156, but it
needs re-emphasis today.

the agent of creation. Some of them refer to events which show that Christ was active in Old Testament days (e.g. 1 Cor. 10: 4), although it must be admitted that this is far from being a central theme. All of them look forward to the completion of the work of Christ at His second coming when He wins His final victory over evil and His people enter into the fulness of salvation. And between the first coming and the second coming He is not inactive, seated on a heavenly throne far from mankind. He is their intercessor with the Father, and they are joined to Him in a spiritual fellowship sustained by the power of His Spirit. This is the New Testament doctrine, and it is essentially one and unified.

At the same time, we have been able to observe that the aspects of the work of Christ which are foremost in the various New Testament documents are quite varied. It is an education for the preacher and pastor to see how the different authors select those elements in the work of Christ which were most relevant to the needs of their audiences. The early preachers found themselves devoting most attention to the resurrection as the proof that Jesus was the divinely appointed and vindicated Messiah. Teachers concerned to instruct the young churches in Christian behaviour inevitably emphasized the exemplary aspects of Christ's work and repeated His teaching. Those who were faced by recalcitrant sinners drew their attention to the certainty that Christ would come as judge, and stressed the enormity of sinning against the One who had bought sinners with His blood. Christians who faced persecution were encouraged by the thought that they were called to the privilege of sharing both Christ's sufferings and His glory. Those who were tempted to turn aside from the faith were given proof that apart from Christ there could be no salvation; He was God's last word to men.

A further point of importance is that we were able to understand the New Testament teaching only by constant recourse to the Old Testament. A rich variety of imagery drawn from that source was used to express the various aspects of the work of Christ. In Christ all the promises of God, given to His people in the religious institutions of Israel (such as the sacrificial system) and in the teaching of the prophets, came to fulfilment. Indeed we may speak of them being more than fulfilled, for it became obvious that time and again the Old Testament imagery was a true but inadequate vehicle to bear all the weight of meaning which the New Testament writers wished to impose upon it.

Now it is true that particularly within the last century scholars have investigated the possible sources of New Testament thought in many other places, in Jewish writings of all kinds, in Greek philosophers, and in the many pagan religions and cults of the ancient world. Considerable light has been thrown upon the meaning of the New Testament for its first readers by these studies, and it would be folly for the scholar to ignore them. In a non-technical presentation such as this book, direct reference to such work has been almost completely neglected, although the results have not been overlooked. What is interesting is that it has proved possible to give a coherent account of New Testament teaching without referring at every point to Philo or gnosticism, and this suggests that the main background and inspiration of the New Testament writers is to be found in the Old Testament. It was the inspired and divinely prepared background for the coming of Christ in a way in which pagan sources never could be. No doubt a full-length presentation of our subject would take into account all these sources and the result would be a much better picture of the New Testament teaching, showing how it leaned upon and how it differed from its cultural environment, but, so far as a basic understanding of the New Testament is concerned, it may fairly be claimed that the Old Testament is the essential piece of background reading.

Another point of great significance is that it has proved possible to show that the New Testament writers present a unified doctrine of the work of Christ which is a legitimate development of the ideas taught by Christ Himself. We are far from pretending to have *proved* that this is the case; the authenticity of the individual statements of Christ is so much under fire in certain quarters today that a minute examination of the text would be necessary in order to substantiate our case. Nevertheless, in an exposition which has sought to examine the texts honestly and without twisting their meaning, we believe that there are the makings of a case that the New Testament writers were witnesses to a common theology based ultimately on what Jesus said and did in His earthly life.

In these various ways we submit that there is to be found one basic New Testament doctrine of the work of Christ, rich in content, to which each of the main New Testament writers makes his own characteristic contribution. But at this point, having set out the New Testament material as objectively as possible, we must face a further question.

Symbols and Reality

It would no doubt be rash and presumptuous for an author to claim that his book is so simple and comprehensible that all his writers ought to be able to understand it without any difficulty. What we do wish to claim, however, is that the teaching of the New Testament about the work of Christ is simple and comprehensible even to the modern reader. Our study has shown that the New Testament writers one and all express the meaning of the work of Christ by means of a variety of pictures, metaphors and symbols. It seems reasonable to suggest that for the most part these means of expression were readily intelligible to their first readers. The language used was that with which they were familiar from the experiences of daily life and from their knowledge of the Old Testament. This is not of course to deny that the New Testament would contain things hard for them to understand; after all it does deal with the most sublime theme known to man. What matters is that the basic points would be within the comprehension of the reader.

It is surely, however, also true that the meaning of the New Testament teaching about the work of Christ ought to be clear to the modern reader. Some of the imagery used is that which all generations of men have found meaningful and which they still use. To speak of Christ as the Light of the World or to express the result of His death in terms of forgiveness should occasion no difficulty to the modern reader. Other types of imagery can likewise readily be made intelligible. For example, a modern city-dweller may not appreciate the tremendous significance attached to water as the means of sustaining life until there is an accident to a local reservoir or aqueduct, but it is possible for him to enter imaginatively into the experience of the dweller in the desert and come to understand sympathetically some of the emotional and elemental content of the offer of Jesus to bestow the water of life upon the thirsty. Similarly, figures of speech and ways of thought which belong to the ancient Near East can be explained for modern man. He may not, for example, be accustomed to ancient ideas of sacrifice, but he can be instructed in how sacrifice was understood in biblical times and so be enabled to see what aspect of the work of Jesus is comprehended in these terms.

It may, therefore, be fairly claimed that in principle the language used in the New Testament is, or can be made, comprehensible to modern man. This is not to say, of course, that in order that a man may understand the gospel we must begin by instructing him in ancient ideas of sacrifice and then expound the meaning of the cross to him in these terms. The example of the New Testament itself clearly proves that the gospel must be preached in contemporary language which will be familiar and understandable. The gospel was offered to first-century men by using imagery that they could readily understand from their cultural background. We are, therefore, fully justified in presenting the gospel today in contemporary language – hence the legitimacy and indeed the inescapable necessity of using a Bible translated into twentieth-century English – and with the aid of imagery that is readily intelligible. Every time that a preacher uses some illustration drawn from everyday life, he is attempting to do precisely this. A preacher who eschewed such illustration and insisted on simply repeating the imagery of the Bible would be placing an unnecessary stumbling-block in the way of his hearers. One does not need to know about "the ashes of a heifer" (Heb. 9: 13) to understand that Christ can save men from sin!

What is more important and controversial is whether the meaning behind the New Testament imagery is essential for us today. What is the status of this language? Is it, for example, a mythological way of speaking, a way of referring to spiritual realities which can be profoundly misleading? This is the opinion of such scholars as Rudolf Bultmann who would dismiss much of the New Testament teaching about the work of Christ as myth and offer their own interpretation of what they believe the myths were trying to express.[2]

We are not concerned here to enter into dialogue with scholars like Bultmann who implicitly or explicitly deny the authority of Scripture in their theology. But within the context of a theology which is based upon Scripture the kind of question which is posed in its most radical form by Bultmann cannot be ignored. In what sense is the New Testament language authoritative for us? We would suggest that the ways in which the New Testament describes

[2] R. Bultmann's famous essay on demythologizing the New Testament appeared in English in H. W. Bartsch (ed.), *Kerygma and Myth* (1954). For a full-scale, reliable and sympathetic account of his thought see W. Schmithals, *An Introduction to the Theology of Rudolf Bultmann* (1968), and for a critical assessment see D. Cairns, *A Gospel without Myth?* (1960).

the death of Jesus are usually metaphorical and symbolical, but the symbolism and the reality are so closely bound up with each other that it would be a hazardous business to attempt to separate the reality from the biblical expression of it. The important point that emerged from our earlier study was that the same basic language of sacrifice, redemption, reconciliation and victory occurred throughout the New Testament. Even when addressing themselves to Gentiles, the biblical writers still used the same Old Testament language to describe the work of Christ. These symbols consequently have scriptural authority for us. As used in the New Testament they express what was believed to be of supreme significance in the work of Christ, and we cannot dispense with them. We must constantly return to them in order to test and validate whatever other imagery that we may care to use in presenting the gospel in modern terms. To abandon biblical language is to abandon the reality which it expresses.

Some of the language is clearly to be taken less literally than the rest. To use the concept of reconciliation as a description of our personal relationship with God is a more adequate means of expression than, say, to picture heaven as a replica of the tabernacle in the wilderness. The former use of language is literal, the latter is metaphorical, but each has its own contribution to make towards the biblical understanding of the work of Christ.

The ultimate question is whether a person is prepared to accept what the New Testament says about the meaning of the work of Christ. A person governed by a so-called scientific approach may wish to deny the possibility of the resurrection of Christ or of His coming at the end of the world. He may claim that there is no room for such events within his world view. The New Testament teaching, however, suggests that such a world view may need revision, not in the interests of stifling truth and producing a blind obscurantist approach to reality, but rather in order that one may do justice to the kind of phenomena which normally (and rightly) lie outside the scope of the scientist.[3]

More serious is the attitude of the person who disputes the realities which are everywhere presupposed by the New Testament doctrine of the work of Christ, namely the fact of human sin and the fact of a God 'with whom we have to do'. The teaching of the

[3] See Karl Heim, *Christian Faith and Natural Science* (1953) and *The Transformation of the Scientific World View* (1953) on these points.

New Testament is that sin is a grim reality, exerting its sway in the hearts of all men, that men are answerable for their sin to God, and that the ultimate result of sin is death. If God is righteous – and the demands of human moral consciousness confirm the biblical revelation that this is His character – then there can be no room in His presence for the sinner. In Christ He has provided "the remedy for the defilement of our sins" (1 Jn. 2: 1 NEB); H:s love has given us a Saviour who delivers us from sin and its consequences, and the unanimous verdict of the New Testament writers is that it is by the death and resurrection of Jesus that we are delivered from sin. We are fully justified in saying more. The way in which the concepts of sacrifice, redemption and substitution pervade the New Testament teaching on the death of Christ indicates that He took our sinfulness upon Himself, He died in our place, He paid a price that we might be delivered. God in Christ Himself dealt with the problem of our sin. These are the realities which are implicit in the language of the New Testament, and which can hardly be expressed without using this or similar terminology. One fears that the reason why the terminology and the reality expressed by it are sometimes toned down or even jettisoned is that men have failed to realize the gravity of human sin or dispute the righteousness and the love of a God who both takes sin seriously and offers a remedy for it. Such an attitude is hard, if not impossible, to justify. For if the teaching of the New Testament is anything like the outline of it given above, this is how God has revealed Himself to us, and there is no other revelation. God acts with perfect justice and with perfect love, so that there can be no grounds for moral criticism of His ways. There remains only the fact of human pride which cannot accept the verdict of God upon sin or allow itself to be saved by what Christ has done. The title of this chapter is *Christ and us*, not *Christ and we*, for the essence of Christianity is that we receive what Christ has done for us, or rather, we receive Him as our Saviour and Lord.

What is true of the beginning of the Christian life is true of its whole course. We are continually debtors to Christ and what He does for us. This is not to say that He does not call us into His service; He may even bid us to share His sufferings. But the fundamental attitude which He requires of us is faith, humble and trusting acceptance of the Lord who died for us. Thus the work of Christ controls the whole content of the Christian life, and the person who makes it his concern to know Christ, as He is revealed in the New

Testament writings, will find that he is not simply amassing a body of factual information but is coming into closer fellowship with the Saviour who is continually doing His work in and for Him.

To think of the work of Christ in this way could just possibly lead to a feeling of pride; if Christ did and does all this for us, what important people we must be. Important we are, but to Him. There is no ground for self-importance or pride. For the ultimate aim of the work of Christ is that there should be a people prepared for God, zealous for good works and living for His glory. Like their Saviour, they will make it their aim to glorify God, and give Him all the praise for His grace. When this takes place, the work of Christ is complete.

Books for Further Reading

James Denney:
The Death of Christ (reprinted by the Tyndale Press, 1951).

P. T. Forsyth:
The Work of Christ (reprinted by the Independent Press, 1952).

E. M. B. Green:
The Meaning of Salvation (Hodder and Stoughton, 1965).

H. E. Guillebaud:
Why the Cross? (I.V.F., 1946).

L. Hodgson:
The Doctrine of the Atonement (Nisbet, 1951).

A. M. Hunter:
The Unity of the New Testament (S.C.M. Press, 1943).

A. M. Hunter:
Introducing New Testament Theology (S.C.M. Press, 1957).

J. Jeremias:
The Central Message of the New Testament (S.C.M. Press, 1965).

L. Morris:
The Apostolic Preaching of the Cross (Tyndale Press, 1955; 1965[3]).

L. Morris:
The Cross in the New Testament (The Paternoster Press, 1965).

V. Taylor:
Jesus and His Sacrifice (Macmillan, 1937).

V. Taylor:
The Atonement in New Testament Teaching (Epworth Press, 1940).

GENERAL INDEX

INDEX OF SCRIPTURE REFERENCES